The True Story Of David Tuccaro Jr.

BAD TO THE BONE

Marala Scott

BAD TO THE BONE

Bad To The Bone
Copyright © 2013 by David Tuccaro Jr.

All rights reserved. Printed and bound in the United States of America. No part of this book may be reproduced or transmitted in any form by any means, electric or mechanical, including photocopying, recording, or by an information storage and retrieval system --- without permission in writing from the publisher, except by a reviewer, who may quote brief passages in a review. Published by: Seraph Book, LLC.

Cover Design By: Alyssa M. Curry
Copyediting: Alyssa M. Curry
Cover Photos By: Caleb Wilson
Author Photo: Gerry Garcia

ISBN 978-0-9820268-8-5
Library of Congress Control Number: 2013952897

For information regarding special discounts for bulk purchases of this book for educational, gift purposes, as a charitable donation, or to arrange a speaking event, please visit: www.seraphbooks.com

www.davidtuccaro.com
twitter@davidtuccarojr
www.facebook.com/davidtuccaro

It is rare to meet someone with such deep passion for life and love, coupled with an emotional intelligence that extends into the spiritual realm. This is how I envision David. He is one of those rare individuals who in his own right, is a profound teacher of life. He has, through his own journey, been broken down, was lost, found and then transformed. Through his journey he rediscovered his passion and purpose for life and as a result restored his health, gained emotional clarity, and rediscovered his spirituality. This book outlines his journey and will serve as an inspiration for all. I strongly recommend this book for anyone seeking to change and improve their lives. David portrays his experiences so effectively that all will gain from his descriptions. What he describes is that journey we are all seeking; it is the transformation to a better life.

Thank you David, for allowing me to be part of your journey.

–Gary Ruelas, D.O., Ph.D.

"Courage is a rare commodity. And often the test of courage is not to die – but to live. In David Jr.'s case, pain has become a condition of life, not a reason for death. That has been the source of his inspiration. He and I spent most a day together, discussing his health. I soon realized that unlike most of us, he trusts his body, and that is mainly why he will continue to thrive. His story is remarkable. You must always have enough courage to tell yourself that you are important to someone else. In his case, to everyone who has met him appreciated how he has dealt with the realities he faces daily. This is a man to go tiger hunting with."

–Peter C. Newman, Legendary Journalist and Author

"The true test of a man is his ability to remain standing after being challenged. David Tuccaro took Leukemia's best punch and he's still here."

DJ Rob Swift
Legend

"I've known David for some time now, he brings me back to the days of selling mixed-tapes out of the trunk. Meet me in the parking structure at Belle Tera, I'd tell him, and he'd buy records off of me when I'd visit California. God knows what it looks like we are doing. It could look like any street corner hustle but the truth is there is a certain force, a power in this music. When it is pressed on vinyl it almost comes off as a healing crystal or gem. It's a strong bond for those that know. And David believes, as strongly as I do, that these small artifacts can heal. It's almost a religion to us."

Frankie Bones
Godfather of American Rave Culture

Dedication

This book is dedicated to all of the people that have unselfishly helped me get to this point in life. Your love, support and encouragement helped me overcome the most challenging time of my life.

Mum, Dad and Jen you guys gave me the courage to fight this when I ran out. Every time I turned around you were there fighting this battle with me. I love you more than I can express.

Cynthia, Genevieve and Madaline you are the reason I continue to fight! I love you.

To my bone marrow donor and brother Christian Holtmann. Thank you for your generous gift of life. You didn't know who I was but you cared about what I needed in order to live. I am still here because of your undying compassion.

A sincere thank you to all of the bone marrow donors. Your choice to give us another chance at life is immeasurable. You may never know what you've done, but we do.

Humbled and Appreciative,
David Tuccaro, Jr.

Acknowledgements

I have a band of family and friends that have gone above anything I would have imagined to show me I've always mattered to them. There were many others along the way that encouraged me to continue the fight although they may never have known. Additionally, there are loved ones that I have lost that motivated me throughout my life or believed I could beat cancer. Thank you! Uncle Tony, my brother Phil, Jeremy, all of my Doctors and Nurses, Dr. Ruelas, DKMS, the World Bone Marrow Data Registry, Provincial Bone Marrow Registry, the Canadian Blood Services and music!

A Note To The Reader

Throughout the process of David's book being written, I've watched the impact of revealing this story change him in a very inspirational way. It has been nothing less than therapeutic in an unimaginable way. It's a difficult task to dig up painful memories and write about them for everyone to read, but this process has helped him release a tremendous amount of pain. It is meant to help others understand what a cancer patient, their family and friends endure. It will help those beginning this difficult battle to know they can beat cancer too. This book, *Bad to the Bone* can bring the hidden reality of cancer to the surface.

David is learning to live life to his full potential and help change the lives of others by sharing his painful experiences. Each of us takes our journey and makes choices that alter our lives forever. David has joined the forces of many compassionate and dedicated individuals in an effort to address a battle taking lives and affecting millions of men, women and children. Compassion and love can help beat this devastating illness as it has helped David.

David is gripping his second chance at life and making the conscious decision to live passionately knowing he belongs. The beauty of it is that David fits perfectly with me. I am very proud of him and his positive outlook on his future.

With Love,
Cynthia Luce

Introduction

This is life. Take it and craft the best of this opportunity while you can because sooner or later you'll leave here. We all do and at some point, our entire history will unobtrusively evaporate into thin air like we never existed unless we make an investment for it to remain. I've chosen to accomplish this by leaving my imprint hoping to inspire others to do, believe and live with more passion. Sharing your pain, triumphs or significant lessons can help others understand adversity in a way no one else is able to. It may allow someone to see something from a unique perspective they may not have considered. Our lessons are powerful if we take the core message along with the strength that evolved from them and impart knowledge into others.

I never fully appreciated the value of my existence until the reality of not being here any longer was hurled at me in the most unsuspecting way. As most people are when something unforeseen happens, I was blindsided and hit with bone chilling news that would affect me for the rest of my life, however long it would be. The problem was, prior to the news, I was already lost inside of my own descending life, walking dead.

I was one of those people meandering through life attempting to be inconspicuous while executing no real plan. Sure, I existed but I wasn't living because I hadn't invested in anything. If I had, some of the recklessness I engaged in would not have occurred. I made choices without giving credence to what anyone thought and I genuinely didn't care if the world watched the mistakes I made. No one seemed to care. When the time came, I'd take flight for a while, land again, drift aimlessly and then continue trudging through life searching for a place I might become a part of something. The thing is, once I took flight it didn't matter where I disembarked as long as I'd find a temporary haven to fit. It never took long for me to realize I didn't belong and once I did, I'd take off again. For the most part, I'd consciously make an effort not to drift into anyone's way or draw attention to myself although I thought it was pretty hard not to notice me.

I'm a six-foot-three, *bad to the bone* Mikisew Cree First Nation. The Cree were the dominant First Nations people in Ft. McMurray, Canada, my home. I have black hair most of the time, brown eyes and a colorful display of history adorning my body in the form of art, which is my way of communicating my story. Every bit of ink has some type of significant narration about a critical point in my lifetime. I can't always talk about what I'm going through or formulate the appropriate words to accurately describe what I want to say. When I do, I seem to make things worse so instead, I've learned to say what others need to hear and for anyone that observes them, I let my tats talk. They reveal a few of my deepest secrets and they're somewhat displayed in code. No one would ever be able to decipher precisely what my ink expresses unless they ask me. And I'm quite capable of discerning sincerity when someone's in a quest to know; simply by the way they ask. It's likely I won't divulge everything but I will explain the general meaning behind my tats. I doubt it completely makes sense to anyone, but I keep a record of my life and wear it on the outside since no one can ever tell what's going on inside of me. There's not much other than an abysmal black hole constantly churning, waiting to house more pain and ambiguity. I don't expect anyone to understand me because I don't quite understand myself, therefore, I'm certain my parents or sister can't either. Until now I've never admitted it, but I wish they did because it's lonely realizing they don't. Tattoos allow me to relocate some of my internal pain to my exterior, as I've become quite the collector. My storage is filled to capacity so at times I have no alternative but to wear it as ink.

My history thus far isn't too good, but it's mine. I choose to own it because it's all I really possess. Retaining as much history in the form of secrets as I've managed made it imperative for me to find a way to express what I believed. The downside is holding it captive can be damaging; and it has been for me.

I don't understand why we encounter so much ugliness, sickness and darkness in this world. I find it difficult to digest the fact that this is the way it is. My own life is a bit of a mystery because I haven't figured it out yet. However, it's trying to figure me out with the barrage of challenges I've been slammed with. I've hit the pavement so hard my bones hurt. I don't know why I keep getting right back up.

The majority of the time I felt like I was standing on the edge looking in at my life or expecting to fall out of it. Since I'm still here, life hasn't lost me in its convoluted narrative. When a dark storm arises with gusting winds, sheets of rain slicing through the air and wails of thunder angrily prepared to emit deafening sounds; I buckle down and take whatever comes. It wasn't long ago I encountered something so vile and vicious I didn't think I'd survive. I had to wake up from the trance I was in and fight with everything in me. The strange thing is I never knew I had it in me to beat anything, let alone this monster. If I didn't learn how to fight for my life, I wouldn't be here today. In order to win, I had to make a choice to stop hiding from reality, decide to live and then prove it by fighting. Regardless of what you've been faced with, there's always a little more fight in you, even if you get down to the reserves. This time, I couldn't hide or outrun it. I was forced to face it and then engage in a merciless battle because if I didn't with certainty, I'd die. I was told that I needed a miracle to survive this.

Here's my story ...

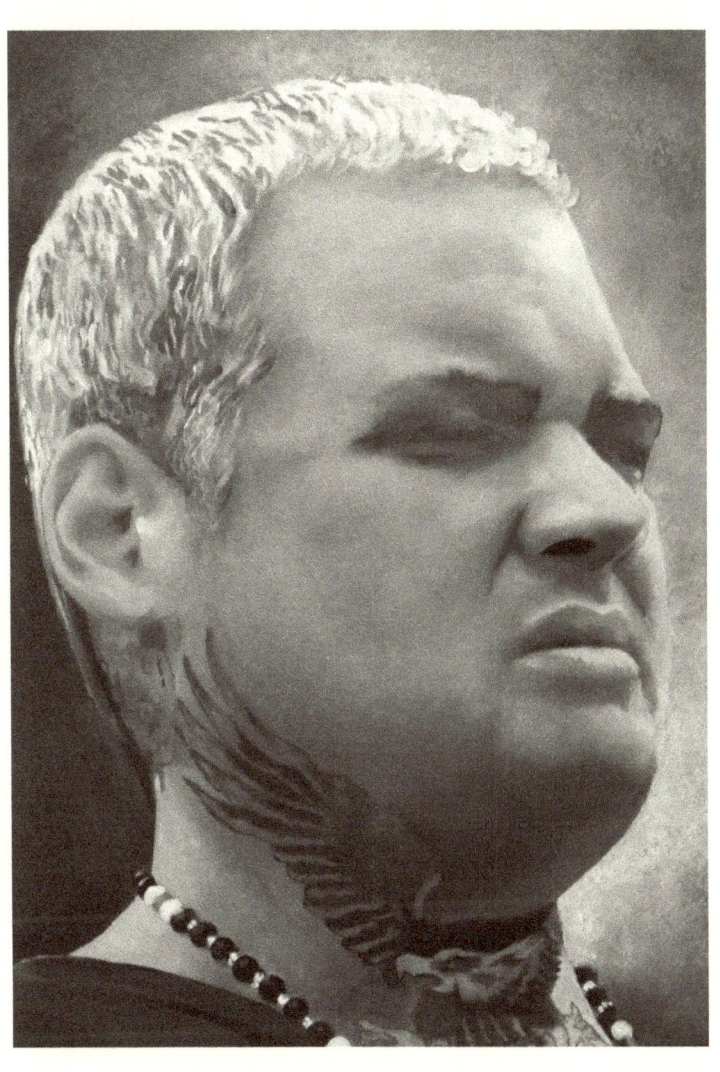

By David George

Chapter 1

A Big Word For An Even Bigger Disease

The small, sterile room was cold and void of everything familiar to me except a faithful stream of negative emotions loosely drifting about. I was lying in an uncomfortable bed swaddled in fear and I couldn't fathom why. It was Christmas Eve in 2006 and I wasn't feeling well. Instead of being excited about spending time with my family, the physical pain I experienced turned agonizing and became such a major distraction, I couldn't think of anything else. Trying to sleep in the depressing darkness, which filtered in an eerie stillness, was impossible. Constant deliberations of worry paced through my congested mind and ignited my fear. Of all the places I wanted to be, this wasn't one of them.

Around two in the morning the noise from the curtain separating my bed from the next startled me. It was briskly yanked open from left to right making a loud screeching sound. The doctor took a couple of steps inside my sectioned off part of the room and planted himself directly in front of me. I pulled myself up to a sitting position and gave him my full attention. After an elongated gaze, his expression became perplexed before sharing his unemotional communication about the discoveries stated on the medical chart he held in his hand.

As if he'd done this a thousand times, the doctor firmly explained my test results. He said they ran three separate blood counts on me and each one indicated my white blood cell count had become worse. In his banter of medical terminology to describe what was wrong I heard one big word that hurled me into complete disarray for a few moments. Stunned, upon realizing *I had it*, absolute terror poured into me. *Leukemia* slipped from between his lips, causing everything else he said to dissolve into nothingness. I felt absolutely helpless, sitting in bed; wearing a blue hospital gown. Nothing came out of my mouth and my face robotically fell into a neutral position. I responded by returning a blank expression while attempting to digest my unexpected and forbidding fate. *Yes, leukemia was a big word for an even bigger disease.*

My initial reaction dwindled and I don't know what I felt other than a profound numbness upon hearing I had *late stage three, leukemia*. Now that *I* had cancer, I didn't know what to expect. Can they treat it? Am I going to get worse? Is this terminal? What happens now? I had a plethora of questions, but I wasn't sure I was ready to ask, so I nodded and remained quiet. Once the oncologist left the room I took a deep breath before trying to make sense of the unsettling report. How did I get leukemia?

For the past few months, I noticed the incessant patterns of frailty my body displayed. There were obvious signs something was extremely wrong. Nonetheless, I didn't consider it to be anything remotely close to leukemia and I certainly didn't know anyone that would have.

I was twenty-five years young and my life hadn't come close to taking off yet. At that moment, the only thing on my mind was my future, which caused me to wonder if I'd have one. Trying to fathom how this ensued, I allowed my dark brown eyes to flutter shut and absorb the darkness with little puddles of water resting beneath my eyelids. Freely allowing it to consume me by going deeper than I imagined, a deadening heaviness followed and occupied my entire body. The flavor of this ominous obscurity made its way to my palate where I tasted the bitterness of fear. I wondered if this would be *a slow death, immense decay.*

A short while later, interrupting my dejected thoughts, was the sound of the curtain being pulled back again. I opened my eyes and glanced over to find my slender, five-foot-seven Mum entering the room. Appearing frustrated with the uncertainty of my condition, she sat in the blue chair next to my bed and crossed her legs. Using a selection of delicate words, I communicated exactly what the doctor told me. Once Mum heard the word leukemia, her eyebrows scrunched together, shock covered her face and she became noticeably upset. Her intense wince made me uncomfortable, like I did something wrong. Then, she displayed a long disapproving stare as though it was implausible for cancer to be a diagnosis. Without warning, Mum unconsciously lashed out at me in complete disbelief breaking free of her typical stoic demeanor.

"Did you tell the doctor to say that? Are you making this up?" she retorted frantically, while brushing her blond hair off the side of her face. Her angry, yet beautiful green eyes became more visible.

I understood I had leukemia, but I didn't know exactly what it was or what it would do to me. Taken aback by her aggressive reaction I replied in a defensive manner with what little tenor I could muster, "No Mum! What's leukemia?"

Without spewing another word of disbelief, she got up and stormed out the room, brushing against the curtain. She left me alone in the room, downright baffled and more afraid than I already was.

Approximately an hour later, Mum returned looking a bit shaken, with my doctor composedly in tow. His voice was resolute as he informed us it was time to go. They had a medevac waiting to take me to Vancouver General Hospital. Without a lengthy exchange of dialogue the inference was clear. Being transported by air implied I needed more extensive care than they were able to provide.

I've never felt time pass so fast or decisions being made as expeditiously as they were on my behalf. Everything was happening quickly; I didn't have time to make sense of anything. I was simply being led through the process without providing an ounce of input for the decisions being made about my healthcare. Sadly, it alluded that there weren't any options.

In the midst of everything going on, I took another glimpse at Mum. I could tell her mind was swirling in a mass of thick turmoil, unable to handle the news well. She was completely freaking out but doing everything she could to contain it, at least while in my presence. Her confident posture shifted, causing her to appear deflated, defeated and at a loss for comforting words. My heart ached for Mum. My heart was aching for *every* Mum forced to bear this.

The pain throughout my body was overwhelming because everything hurt. I sat in bed nervously biting my fingernails; impatiently waiting to find out what the doctors next move would be since *I* didn't have one.

When the doctor came to check on me he explained more about my illness. He told me the best candidates of leukemia are children because their systems are more responsive so they're able to get a higher rate of full remission and recover better. However, I wasn't a child and those statistics weren't applicable to me.

Next, he had the cumbersome task of communicating the weighty implications regarding my situation. My cancer was bad, the diagnosis was extremely poor because the damage was already done and I needed intense treatment as quickly as I could get it.

By 5:30 a.m. I was tightly strapped onto a metal gurney, rolled down the long cold hospital corridor, put into an ambulance and driven to the airport. All I could think of was, *I have cancer.*

While the EMT's were trying to lift me onto the plane they refused to let Mum on board. Though it caused a major problem, I knew that plane wasn't taking off without her and somehow, she got on. I stared out the window of the plane and watched the sun rising over the mountains as we ascended higher. A strange peacefulness invaded my thoughts and I said to myself, "If I die, I'm glad this is the last thing I'll see."

As we reached Vancouver, dense pillows of grey and black clouds shrouded the beautiful rising sun, then released a heavy rainfall that fell like darts into the snow. Once the plane landed, they quickly unloaded me like I was ready to detonate and then rushed me into the emergency room where a team of doctors had prepped for my arrival. The room felt like the inside of a refrigerator, it was sterile and somewhat morbid. Without prior introduction, one of the doctors stepped closer to me and lifted the white blanket off my waist. He wiped my hip off with a damp swab and without further explanation said, "You're going to feel a little pressure." Before I could respond, a long needle was inserted deep into my hip. To alleviate a loud moan from forcing its way out, I clenched my teeth together and tightly gripped the edge of the bed. The digging and pushing from the needle produced a constant surge of intolerable pain. Afterwards, I found out he completed a hip biopsy. For the next few hours, they ran several tests and checked my blood again. I didn't understand the severity of my condition; nevertheless, I had a strong notion it wasn't going to improve.

When they were done with me, one of the attendants carefully guided my gurney down a hallway, onto the elevator and up to the fifteenth floor. After stopping at the nursing station, he rolled me into the room I'd occupy until the doctors figured everything out. I didn't know if he thought I was afraid or not, but I was. He said my nurse would be in shortly and then made a quiet exit.

While trying to find a comfortable position in bed, I overheard Mum talking to the doctor that had been taking care of me since I arrived. Communicating as though Mum should've expected it, she said, "We don't have much hope he'll make it through the night." Before shuddering off the initial feeling of shock, I remember inhaling, but I don't recall how long it was before that terrified breath came out. My Christmas present in 2006 was the threat of death and Mum's, the threat of losing her son.

Mum nervously slipped through the curtain with the color flushed from her beautiful face. I could discern the panic in her moderately glassy eyes before they were drawn to the floor. Appearing as though she was trying to suppress what the doctor told her, she returned to my bedside. With an empathetic touch she ran her hand across my leg and then quietly sat in the chair next to me. Mum didn't know what to say and I could hardly imagine what she was thinking. I didn't have a clue how any of this transpired so quickly and I was certain she didn't either. My expression fell vacant and I emptied of everything except fear. The aggressive rhythm of a powwow drum controlled my heartbeat. I wasn't done with my life and I didn't want to die like this. I turned to face Mum and asked with teary eyes, "So when do I expire?" As Mum lifted her head towards me, I detected her deep sadness. It had risen to the surface of her eyes filling them with heavy tears. Without replying, she turned away and stared out the window.

Early that afternoon, a spiritual counselor came by to visit me. I could sense she wanted to give me my last rites so I politely asked her to leave the room. I decided I'd be the one to determine when it was time to give up. I wasn't willing to accept a stranger telling me I was *done,* without knowing if I wanted to fight for my life. I wasn't happy with the situation but I wasn't hopeless either. You don't just give in and forfeit because death is pounding on your door.

    I became enraged and everything faded to black as I ascended into my childhood memories to revisit them before it was too late.

Chapter 2

Canadian Life

I never really thought about the number of people that were like me or considered how many others had the same blood flowing through their veins. We all have some type of history and our bloodline reveals more of the narration than you think. The problem is, until something happens, we really don't know what that is.

Although I'm alive, I've been allowing life to pass through me because I really wasn't going through it. When I think back at the time I've squandered, not making use of such a tremendous gift, I can only shake my head in disbelief and disgust. I'm a soft-spoken kind of guy that has more thoughts than spoken words. I withhold most opinions while my true feelings are buried deep inside of me like the bitter cold of Canada.

I love Canada. It's where I was born and spent the majority of my life. More importantly, it's where my father poured out a lifetime of sweat equity and invested himself in not only his companies but also the community and people in it. Canada is rooted inside of me and even more profoundly inside of my father. It's where my history is, story begins and the place where my life changed forever.

Growing up in Northern Canada provided the natural backdrop of lush fragrant forests for hiking, in addition to, wide streams for abundant fishing, boating and various water activities during the summer. Living there meant adjusting to countless days cheated out of sunlight by the darkness and expecting a sharp cutting wind combined with blistering cold in the winter. The merciless weather could easily kill anyone unprepared for its brutality. Regardless of the secrets the weather reserved, the scenery could never be bound to any kind of restraints. The Canadian landscape is nothing less than majestic with its rushing streams, towering summits, hot springs and ice fields amidst the beautiful scenic snow-capped peaks. The snow always seemed to generously lend itself to an abundance of adventurous outdoor activities, as long as you're able to handle the temperatures. It's rather difficult when you're working in it.

The winter months in Ft. McMurray usually sustained a silent demand that caused Dad to keep a truckload of firewood on hand in case one of the many snowstorms knocked out the power and robbed us of our warmth. The worst possible chores to have were outside, during the winter. When a load of firewood was dropped off someone had to stack it on the side of the garage. After a blizzard or heavy snow blew through, typically mounting several feet high, the driveway needed to be found and shoveled. My younger sister Jennifer lucked out because even though we're only thirteen months, twelve days and sixteen hours apart, naturally, Dad assigned those responsibilities to me.

It was normal for the temperature to exceed -44 Celsius making it absolutely impossible to venture outside without protecting my body. I'd wear several layers of warm clothing beneath my thick down parka along with a heavy pair of gloves to shield my hands from frostbite. Long before I began the work, I found myself mentally exhausted at the mere thought of it. After stalling as long as I could, I'd slip into my Sorel insulated boots and grab my hat. Carrying an edge of reluctance, I'd head into the bitter cold just to chip away a thick layer of ice off of the driveway with a small garden tool. Although I was thirteen at the time, the rigid air seemed to suck the life out of me like a vacuum. I kept a wool scarf wrapped securely around my nose and mouth while working as quickly as possible. It would have been arduous for anyone to breathe because the cold was overly intense. For some reason, it didn't matter what I was wearing. The icy chills quickly penetrated each layer of clothing and triggered uncontrollable shivering throughout my body. Under those conditions, it was virtually impossible to finish the entire driveway in less than two days. I spent a great deal of time darting inside the house just to get my body back to normal.

Throughout my teenage years, I became fairly active in sports and participated on a regular basis, which ended up being nine months out of the year. Playing hockey on a frozen pond or in the street with friends was something I refused to turn down. Rugby, working out and cross-country training were all fun, however, the highlight of any day was spending time in the picturesque Canadian Rockies. Being present in the spectacular panoramic scenery brought about an incredible responsiveness to nature, especially while snowboarding, which I loved more than anything.

Going up the ski lift was just as exhilarating as coming down the mountain. It offered time to appreciate the breathtaking view of the dense lines of snow-capped trees combined with the thick white blanket covering the mountains that punched through the sky. I didn't want to think about anything else.

As soon as my feet were strapped onto the snowboard I was eager to begin my journey down the extraordinarily scenic mountain path. Absorbing the thin rays of sunlight peeking through the trees was equivalent to life-saving medicine running through my veins. My typically clouded head instantly became as finely tuned as it could possibly get upon my descent. Once I hit a graceful speed, my body thoughtlessly steered itself from left to right. I generously dusted the powder allowing a white wave to spray liberally behind me. An irrepressible stream of adrenaline didn't take much to break free because I was surrounded by the inspiration. I needed to release it. It became a flawless outlet to realign my keen awareness and it worked. This was one of the best experiences I had living in Canada.

By the time I reached high school there was another scenario that helped shape my life. When it was presented, I didn't fully appreciate the opportunity my father placed in front of me because I hadn't figured anything out. I struggled with an inability to develop any real sense of direction at that point because I didn't know who I was or where I belonged. The uncertainty created a tremendous amount of internal stress. Dad took notice and decided to send Jen and I to Shawnigan Lake School on Vancouver Island, which is the largest boarding school in Canada. He wanted us to select a school that we'd be happy with so he told Jen and I to find one. Dad's objective was for us to have exposure to the best education and he preferred it to be at a school offering cultural diversity. My father was an advocate for education and proved it by investing heavily into ours.

I thought going away to school would provide the opportunity for me to gain more independence. To the contrary, it didn't take long before I discovered adapting to the environment proved to be relatively difficult. I made friends and hung out with a lot of associates; nevertheless, no one actually knew what was going on in my head. I got the impression most of the other students didn't care to network with me, but I wasn't exactly beaming with confidence like the majority of them. I used humor to disguise my insecurities and sometimes it worked.

Boarding school consisted of a completely different environment than that of a typical school. It was very structured and presented an unyielding platform. The kids seemed to gravitate more towards people most like themselves, yet I didn't meet anyone like me. Although I tried, I didn't feel like I could be myself at Shawnigan Lake, which caused me to miss home even more. As for my sister, she fit right in.

The campus had over three hundred impeccably manicured acres offering everything necessary to pursue personal excellence and I didn't belong there. I was exceedingly self-conscious and often worried the other kids wouldn't like me. When they didn't, I honestly couldn't ascertain the reason. I owned a cyclic feeling of self-defeat coupled with a biting loneliness that wouldn't disappear, regardless of how hard I tried to overcome it. To make it worse, I missed my Mum.

Mum and I were awfully close and she understood me as much as it was possible for anyone to. By sending care packages, she tried to help me adapt so I wouldn't feel lonely. When I opened the box, my eyes lit up with excitement and it wasn't because of the noodles, soups and little things she sent to help me get by. It was because she was thinking about me. Mum always put a bag of glitter inside the card and when I opened it, a huge mess emptied all over the floor. She knew how to make me smile. I realized I still needed her guidance, laughter and more than anything, her beautiful presence. It was comforting to be around Mum and I missed that. Unlike anyone else, she was a free spirit and I felt exactly the same way around her.

I wasn't sure how the other kids handled being away from home because I didn't like it. And once I decided I didn't want to be there, little things that typically wouldn't bother me became magnified. In an attempt to lessen the threat of loneliness, I began a desperate search to find some semblance of who I was. Inherently, I found it inside of the vast domain of music where I didn't feel judged or inadequate.

When it came to music I was free to hear what I wanted and felt what I needed. Music took something out of me, but returned something better in its place. It didn't take long before I embraced the soul of music all the way to its history. It became the only thing I completely understood and it understood me.

Whenever I needed to break away from the rest of my life and unearth something good in mine, without fail, music delivered. It brought about an immediate euphoric sense of happiness while removing the silent misery and dejected feeling that incessantly tried to claim me.

It was fascinating to dive inside of music and find myself away from everything without feeling a need to think about whatever was going on in my life. It's not like I had a bad childhood or anything, but it bothered me that people didn't understand why I should have anything wrong with me. The truth of it is; if you're not happy, sometimes you're just not happy. Often, people search for a reason why someone's unhappy but that doesn't mean there's always an identifiable origin to sadness. Just because something was going on with me, didn't infer Mum, Dad or Jennifer was the cause. Most of the time, no one knew what was wrong with me, including me.

I found music to be a healthy escape that has a way of taking me away from everything by providing a cavernous area I'm inherently able to thrive in. It's liberating from a bad day and delivers me from the pain of sheer loneliness. One of the most captivating aspects is the lyrics talk to me in a way no one else can, and some of them have a way of repairing me when I'm broken. I frequently found lyrics that expressed my emotions and ideologies to perfection.

Reminiscent of my early childhood, music was naturally infused into my daily life until it finally made its way completely inside of me. Casually, its melodious sounds drifted throughout our house in a relaxed sort of way, leaving a perceptible sense of belonging. For some people, food provides comfort while for others it may be sports, movies, art or whatever they find to help disengage from reality. In our house, music was that thing. Having an element, which brings people together can contribute to constructing a bond between them. Music was ours.

My sister loved anything in the Top 40. Dad was synonymous with the sounds of the Eagles while he and Mum shared an interest in the great songs of Motown. My grandpa, Mum's dad, played all types of lively finger popping swing and jazz. He seemed to know everything about music and possessed Mum's enthusiasm for the sounds of Motown. Music surrounded all of us.

I loved the hair-raising sensation I felt when I heard a specific note and the spine tingling that originated from feeling the unbelievable soul grabbing lyrics. Regardless of how hard I try to explain what music does to me, it's implausible to articulate what it feels like in a manner that will do it justice.

Since I appeared to be trapped in an introverted and rather shy state, music was the key to bringing about a communicative freedom. Essentially, it became my approach to meet people and it worked. I leveraged my extensive knowledge of music as an avenue to converse and managed to have gratifying, relationship-building conversations. I loved all types of music with the exception of country. It didn't mean country wasn't good; it was that my palate predominately required rock and a lot of it. I preferred my music to be loud, have evocative lyrics so I could sing along and the riff had to be a killer.

Music knows how to hold my attention like nothing I've ever experienced. Most of the time, it takes me on a mental journey, trailing the direction of the music until I end up wherever it lands, usually in a better place.

There was one lone road leading in and out of Ft. McMurray. Besides the panoramic view of the countryside, there wasn't much outside of it other than the reserves. In the literal sense, Ft. McMurray made me feel as if I'd become imprisoned behind a large stone wall but at least, I had music.

Since my father was quite notable, I didn't have two parents; instead I had a community looking after me. Though it sounds nice, I found it overwhelming to have people constantly in my business. Obviously, the extra eyes watching made it difficult for me to go anywhere or do much without being monitored. Not that I required it, but I didn't have room to behave roguishly. If I caused trouble, it would've unquestionably effected my father's reputation. I never felt I had one or was respected to begin with, so I didn't have anything to protect. Besides, I never wanted to hurt Dad or embarrass Mum in any way.

The clicking on the metal side rails of my bed garnered my attention. I looked to my left and found the nurse and her assistant preparing me for transport.

Chapter 3

The Destruction Cancer Brings

Everything was moving along like the copious flow of a river. I'd nearly forgotten it was Christmas morning. With my eyes closed, I listened to the rhythmic clicking of the wheels on the bed, until it stopped. I was being taken down to the x-ray department to have a Hickman line inserted by the radiologist.

After being prepped, with expert precision, the line was tunneled under the skin of my chest into a vein. The tip of the tube sat in the large vein right above my heart while the other end of the line hung out of my body from my chest. The line was attached to a drip and had two additional ports so I could receive my chemotherapy along with the stream of medications I'd receive. Systematically I was returned to my room without a word.

When the nurse checked my vitals, I stared out the window and watched the shimmering snowfall before drifting off to sleep. The large flakes were perfect and every one of them, unique.

After a brief drug induced sleep, I woke up with heavy dosages of medication filtering throughout my body. It had already begun. The intravenous delivery of chemo worked rapidly. It was necessary because they were trying to keep me alive as long as possible.

My drowsy eyes came into a gradual focus after rubbing them. When I made a slight tilt of my head upwards, I discovered Dad standing on the side of my bed emitting an involuntary look of apprehension. In an unsuccessful attempt to be reassuring, he stated in his assertive business tone, "You'll be fine in six months." I closed my eyes and allowed his confident words to resonate with me for a brief moment before locking eyes with him again. Although I wanted to believe Dad, I didn't. The dejected expression resting on his bronzed face let me know he didn't believe it either. Dad held his tongue when he didn't know something, which made me certain he was trying to figure out how to stop me from dying. My father had accomplished many things throughout his life, but this one seemed to be the impossible. When I watched him steal a glance at Mum, I could tell it was daunting for him to observe her struggling to hold it together.

Dad had a soft spot when it came to Mum. It always seemed like she internalized her personal agony and let everyone else see her strength, even when it wasn't real. This time I believed both of them were at a complete loss because this was something neither could control.

Things were tough for Dad in recent months on a personal level. He's extremely close to his family and sadly, his father passed away. He buried Grandpa

Gabe in November that year up in Ft. Chipewyan and hadn't completely accepted the loss. I don't think any of us had. With great sorrow, he lost other family members as well. The same way some people wear pain on their face, Dad's was weighing heavily on his heart. I'm not convinced there's ever an appropriate time to accept the loss of someone you love, so my heart continued to ache for him. Unfortunately, I'd just become another emotional burden to my father, as if I hadn't been already.

Dad's substantial heartache was visible prior to my leukemia diagnosis, but I'm certain it created a continuum of mourning evident by the way he walked. His statuesque posture reflected the agony straddling his strong shoulders. Even his eyes presented an immense tale of sadness.

It was difficult watching my father carry a grave disposition because he'd always maintained a robust and timely sense of humor or selected words of wisdom to share. If I asked him anything he thought I needed to learn on my own, his standard advice was, "Figure it out." When I agreed to do something, he was stern in his respect for commitment and reiterated, "If you say you're going to do something, do it!" This time, there was nothing to laugh about, I couldn't figure it out or do anything about it and unfortunately he couldn't either.

Dad's temperate brown eyes studied my grave expression, realizing I wasn't expected to survive. And I couldn't help but observed the profound suffering this brought to my parents. Words alone couldn't possibly pull the degree of pain into a comprehensible summary.

Several hours discreetly slipped by and Dad was gone for the night. I rubbed my hands together to warm them and then reached for the extra blanket on the bottom of the bed to rid myself of the chill. With the exception of the faint beeping coming from the monitor, silence permeated the room. It felt like a mortuary bleeding an eerie stillness while a significant storm was nearly upon us. I imagined the Black Death was combing the corridors of the hospital looking for me but it didn't matter; cancer had already found me.

Allowing her body language to appear quite composed, I knew better. Mum remained in the chair, eyes guardedly upon me, with her hands gripping her upper arms. Cancer was an extreme leap to a disease she would never have imagined. Other than the occasional bronchitis, a cold or the flu, I didn't get sick much.

When I made the slightest sound or movement displaying discomfort, her eyes presented a wave of uneasiness. Without speaking a single word, she transmitted an unnerving silence. I found Mum's nonverbal communication to be just as effective as her verbal.

Even in the midst of a terrible situation, Mum was marked by elegance. Her beautiful, slender face had become frail and strained while her blonde hair, hanging a few inches below her jawline, seemed as lifeless as I felt. Mum hadn't eaten or rested properly since I was admitted to the hospital and it was beginning to show. She put on the mask with a positive facade and worked to conceal her thoughts, but I knew Mum; she was petrified. It didn't help when the hospital staff entered the room wearing their white Hazmat suits to completely sanitize the bathroom every time I used it. I was quickly flooded with cytotoxic drugs and since I was now cytotoxic, it was dangerous for anyone to handle my output. I noticed they were wearing gloves much thicker than the industrial strength rubber gloves to ensure proper protection. Being handled in this manner made me feel less than human and somewhat depressed. The reality of my condition left me descending in quicksand.

As another safeguard, the room pressure was negative to prevent any kind of cross-contamination. There was an inflow of air, but there wasn't any outflow. The hospital did everything possible to create a sterile environment. They were protecting me, as well as others fighting this disease from numerous risks to our health.

Although I understood it was a critical precaution, I couldn't imagine what a child must have felt. The hospital gave the impression as though I was living in a holding cell where they'd already prepared for my passing. And when I did, they'd clean up and get ready for the next person. Handling my illness appeared to be nothing more than a routine. It was a job and what they did every day from one patient to the next. The employees operated as if they had been mentally prepared to handle death as often as it occurred.

A hospital has all of the love in the world with the births and healing that takes place and then it's coupled with an abundance of pain and death. So I viewed it as a revolving door of life and death.

When I glanced at Mum, I wondered what she was thinking about. I called her name, but seemingly distracted, she turned away and looked towards the door as if someone was motioning for her. Without responding to me she got up, stepped out the room and entered the hallway. I heard the doctor reviewing my results, reiterate to Mum the severity of my leukemia. I became incensed because again, she stated I was, "*Going to die,*" and I knew Mum couldn't handle it. Hearing someone say that your child would die only needed to be said *once*. I don't know how any Mum could handle hearing those words!

I paused for a few minutes and let her comments resonate. After attempting to understand her motive for sounding so callous and direct, I realized she had to make Mum accept reality. Mum needed to know and I had to accept it.

Mum's face was pale when she returned to my bedside. After lightly adjusting the blanket covering me she picked up the phone to begin notifying our family members of my condition. It was taxing for me to hear. Listening to Mum give careful consideration to her words, with great sensitivity for each person, proved to be a grueling task.

After speaking with her brother Tony, she reached over and handed me the phone. I could tell by Mum's somber disposition he wasn't taking it well. When I said, "Hello," my word escaped in a low whisper because I could already hear his intense sobbing. It was far more than my heart could handle because Tony and I were close. Everything I loved about music, he loved too. I could talk with him about anything. Tony constantly went out of his way to look out for me. We were close in age and he always made me feel I was important to him, like I actually mattered. Hearing Tony's heart-wrenching sobs ripped me apart. I couldn't take it so I handed the phone back to Mum. Tony's reaction validated what Mum was struggling to hold back.

While the primary focus was being given to me, it didn't take long before I realized my family and friends were automatically invited to go along for the emotionally gripping ride. What it does to them isn't something that's considered or treated. This thing, *cancer*, drags everyone around you inside of it to maximize the damage as much as possible.

Attempting to conceal how terrified I'd become ventured far past challenging. Being faced with death is a scary thing. It brought an immediate appreciation for every single breath I took, along with each beautiful experience I was privileged to share with my family. I was grateful to have my parents help me deal with the emotional ramifications of what seemed to be the final season of my life. I appreciated my baby sister, being there for me, too.

As an unbelievable exhibit featuring the gifts of life that surround us, I've seen a vast amount of natural magnificence in my country, through my travels abroad and with those I love. I've been presented with some of the most astounding opportunities imaginable and more than anything I wanted to be a part of something great, but nothing seemed to work out. Now, the only view I had was the one out my hospital window overlooking a crowded parking lot, being covered with another fresh coat of snow beneath the black winter sky.

Careful not to tug on my Hickman line, I turned to lie on my left side and dragged the white blanket up over my shoulders. I closed my eyes and began to reminisce while my tears escaped. This time, they were much heavier.

Chapter 4

My Family Dynamics

People have the tendency to focus on their own life and forget about other things, which should be important to them, but not Dad. He remained increasingly busy building his companies, but continued to check on me with the occasional questioning of my whereabouts. I don't know how he found the time, but he did. Before I went to Shawnigan Lake, he'd call and ask where I was, usually stating someone told him I was somewhere I shouldn't be. During the times in question, I was either on my way to school, or coming home because there wasn't much to do in Ft. McMurray to begin with. Either he was being lied to or Dad was bluffing just to keep tight tabs on me in his own way. Regardless, it worked. I had too much respect for him to step out of line.

Most of the time it was Mum, Jen and I at home because Dad spent a great deal of time diligently working to establish his presence throughout the community. While constantly working to refine his respectable character, which extended far beyond the boundaries of Ft. McMurray, he carefully crafted his legacy. It was as if Dad knew precisely what he wanted to accomplish, created the plan and worked tirelessly towards his goals until he achieved them. Based on my observation, I've always considered Mum to be that strong woman who worked hard to support my father's efforts.

At some point, everyone needs an uninterrupted supply of encouragement. When your self-esteem is at a low, having someone believe in you can make the difference in achieving your goals. Sometimes, people need a little help standing strong until they've begun to do it consistently on their own by building strength and tolerance for discomfort. Faith can produce tremendous progress in the most inconceivable ways.

What I found inspirational about my father is whatever he did it was to the best of his abilities. He'd dive all in with his heart, strong hands and a distinct plan, ready to make things happen. Since he built a reputation of being consistent with his work ethic, people predicted he'd accomplish his goal and do it better than expected. By all accounts, he did. Dad put forth the effort that displayed his passion and he refused to give in, especially during the most challenging times when he was tested.

Although Dad had numerous accomplishments, it wasn't long before I realized I didn't share the same hunger for the things he enjoyed. He was fervent about golf and played well, while I disliked golf and went out of my way to play terribly so he'd give up on me. I'd take the club and slice the ball so after about ten shots like that I was done. School was incapable of pulling a sustainable appetite out of me and I didn't care to learn the intricacies of his business the way he would have wanted. His companies were developing quite successfully and the opportunity for me to work there remained open. I surmised if I worked with Dad long term I'd be miserable because his vision wasn't my dream.

Hockey was a favorite for most people in Ft. McMurray, let alone Canada, but initially, it wasn't innate to me. The sport didn't pull me onto the ice with a gliding fervor because I wasn't ready to be part of the gongshow and I definitely didn't want to be a duster. Regardless, I was forced to play because Dad played. Yet, for some unforeseen reason I grew to love hockey and spent a lot of time on the ice.

My father was a champion in wrestling and won a gold medal at the Arctic Winter Games. He excelled in hockey, baseball, softball and basketball quite naturally. Dad did exceptionally well in whatever sport he played and that discipline carried over and transcended into his business career. He tried to mold me into what he was athletically; unfortunately I wasn't a natural athlete although I enjoyed specific activities. I was quiet, more like Mum and Grandma Tuccaro.

As time progressed, I didn't connect with my family and I felt like an outsider. I'm pretty reserved or what others call timid and for the most part, my typical demeanor is mild. Being malicious, bullying or bothering anyone isn't part of my character. Some of my extended family members called me names, which made it difficult to put my guard down or be myself around them. Perhaps they didn't think about what they were doing, but ultimately, it was emotionally scarring. Situations like that are what caused me to seek refuge inward even more than I already had and no one seemed to understand why. The way I was treated helped shape my insecurities and caused me to be relatively uptight around people. I didn't like being picked on and have never known anyone that did, so I couldn't figure out why people wanted to be cruel if they wouldn't like the negative behavior returned to them. The ugly nuisances of life can be disheartening when all you want to do is live peacefully.

Other than Uncle Tony, no one took an interest in me for too long. I couldn't understand why people didn't want to connect with me even as time passed, but they didn't. I was quiet, compassionate and genuinely cared more about others than myself but I learned the hard way, none of that mattered. Since I wasn't a natural fit within the family, I felt like the black sheep. I can't explain it but I didn't exactly consider myself to be the type of son Dad really wanted. I thought he would've appreciated someone more like him. He was strong, intelligent, resilient and disciplined. While I always wished I had his qualities, I just didn't. I was different and had to work hard to be me because I wasn't readily accepted. I didn't change, so it must have taken tremendous effort to stay this way, although, unintentional.

No one had any idea of how difficult it was for me to carry the insecurity of not belonging and the pain loneliness supplied along with it. I hid them inside of me, while speculating what the results would ultimately manifest into one day. I wasn't sure what would happen if the simmering, yet harmful emotions ever collided. When I came across others that demonstrated evidence of being afflicted with the same look of despair, I felt sorry for them. I wanted to help them but I didn't know how to help myself.

An incomprehensible facet of my life was the relationship Jen had with my parents in comparison to mine. Jen got away with nearly everything and it seemed as if she was never wrong in my parent's eyes. Even when she was, she wasn't. My sister stayed pretty self-sufficient, which seemed to alleviate my parent's worry about her. She did better than I in school so she managed to have, what I deemed, a more stress-free life. Admittedly, I've caused my share of trouble here and there, although nothing major or memorable, just trivial things like messing around in school because I was desperately trying to fit in. For the most part, when it came to my family I felt like I was looking through a large picture window into their happy life.

While Dad spent time with me he actually paid a lot more attention to Jen, causing me to feel like a disappointment because I wasn't like him. More importantly I discovered they shared a bond I wasn't a part of. It definitely threw a penetrable and harsh blow to my self-esteem. Nonetheless, that's just the way it was. I wasn't able to pinpoint why Dad and I had that disconnect but it was there and reasonably discernible. Perhaps it was because he thought I didn't need anything since I was a guy. I knew his lack of attention wasn't done out of hate or malice, but it was done. I never questioned Dad's love for me but one of the things I wanted most of all was to have a significant bond with him, too.

We traveled a lot as a family, but most of the time Jen and I would normally break off and do our own thing. We found ways to enjoy the vacations on our own. That was fine with me because I preferred the space and I really didn't feel a strong family connection.

One weekend, Dad and I went fishing on Charles Lake in the Northwest Territories. The lake was flanked with an abundance of lush green trees and we were surrounded by a spectacular view. That trip meant the most to me because it was absolutely amazing. We stayed in a basic little cabin that didn't have electricity. There were two little outboard motorboats and the only way into Lake Charles was by floatplane. Dad won the trip in a golf tournament in Ft. McMurray and he chose to take *me*. I felt like his son and it felt great!

The majority of kids I knew didn't want to have anything to do with their parents. But there were quite a few things I needed to learn from Dad that weren't instinctive to me. Dad was a magnet for people and a great communicator. When it came to girls I didn't have a clue where to begin. I found conversing with them terribly awkward and definitely could've used his help. By the time I reached high school I knew I was a lost soul and the timing never connected properly for us to build a healthy father-son relationship. If Dad became upset with me for any reason, my sister jumped on the bandwagon and rode it, leaving me to defend myself. I didn't have anyone to stand up for me, which made it difficult to win. Sometimes, people need to win. Even if they can't, they just need to feel like they can.

My sister had a pretty jaunty personality. When it came to interacting with people or fitting in, Jen didn't have to try because she was always well-liked by everyone. It appeared to be quite fluent for her because she had several of Dad's propensities. Jen was strong-willed and for some reason, garnered a lot of attention from him. They had an unyielding connection. My parents really love Jen and so do I, but I absolutely envied her. It didn't take me long to realize I needed to be on her good side because if I wasn't everyone would turn on me.

Jen had an adventurous spirit. She was athletic, played a few sports and a couple of musical instruments too. I alleged my sister was more than content with her upbringing because for the most part I don't ever remember her getting into trouble.

While my subtle actions eluded everyone, I spent years trying to find myself but never manage to do it. In the society we lived in, I felt like a nomadic free spirit and lived that way. I lost several years going adrift and once I began to do so I picked up momentum allowing the powerful current to take me; and it wasn't against my will.

Things were going much better in school during my senior year. The first few years were a bit jagged. Lacking in focus and unable to academically perform up to their standards nearly caused me to be sent home. I wasn't putting enough into my education. Shawnigan Lake provided us with a superior education in exchange for our academic discipline, passion and attention, which I failed to contribute to so they decided to send me home. Sadly, I didn't give any real opposition either. I believed Jen would continue thriving while I tried to make it work elsewhere. I called Dad and told him what was going on. While disappointed, he agreed to pick me up, but on the weekend we had a big ski trip that I was supposed to attend.

Between the time I called my father and his arrival, there was one teacher that saw *something* in me I hadn't seen in myself. That teacher refused to let me quit and encouraged me to stay and fight because the opportunity my father provided was exceptional. Realizing what I had, I decided to turn things around and put forth the effort. By the time Dad came to retrieve me, I didn't want to go home. I stayed and made it work understanding Shawnigan Lake was more amazing and critical to my development than I initially considered. I was happy I didn't give up and walk away because my relationship with Jen was at its best. That year, the Director gave me an award for academics because of the improvements I made. No one knew it, but it meant more to me than anything. I learned that *I am* capable.

Fighting isn't a behavior innate to my character but this time it was necessary to prove to myself I was worth it. If I didn't, I don't know if I'd ever fight for anything again.

I felt a soft hand gently lift my wrist to check my pulse. Christmas was over and I was still alive. There must be a reason.

Chapter 5

Cause And Effects Of Anger

My eyes fluttered open to the view of white ceiling tiles. Somewhere between consciousness and the medications knocking me out I spent the night thinking, afraid and still in pain. Mum was in the chair, sleeping in what appeared to be a rather uncomfortable position and the sky was just beginning to show signs of light.

The day after Christmas, I acknowledged the fact I was going to die. Avoiding reality could only make things worse since I didn't have control over the situation. I decided I'd do everything the doctors advised so I could live as long as the cancer permitted. I wasn't comfortable with that particular theory and had a hard time accepting it. If I wanted to have hope that didn't feel like a positive perspective to own. However, my doctor was the expert and her approach was, pray for the best but expect the worst. I think everyone was expecting the worst.

In a strange way, I understood the rule of death because it was rather simple; it maintains an aura of inevitability. It's going to happen. Silently, its lingering toxins were adrift inside of me ravishing my interior. Conceding to what the doctor said, and accepting the worst, meant I was giving cancer too much authority over me.

Before drifting in and out of a slumber, whenever I could, I took in as much as possible of Mum, Dad, Jen, family, friends and life as a whole. I absorbed their warmth, smiles, eyes, movements and every little detail I could garner. I never knew if that would be the last time I saw them, heard their voice or felt their touch. Saying goodbye may not have been an option. Whether I went to sleep for the night or took a brief nap, I was surprised each time I woke up.

As the days passed, the doctors and nurses continued treatment. I can't explain why, but one day I experienced the sensation of not being in my body as if I were on the outside looking in. I knew I was in my body, but it seemed like I was observing what they were doing to me, like an unwilling participant. Perhaps it was the combination of powerful medications submerging my system or the fear I was attempting to hide that caused me to be out of sorts. Regardless of the reason, it frightened me because I didn't want to die and it felt like I had.

In the short time frame since being admitted, I reached a volume of having to take twenty-three pills a day. The pills were helping combat the cancer but many of them were doing further damage to other parts of my body. The additional medications were given as an effort to counter those effects. It didn't matter; the doctors were simply buying whatever time they could scrape together.

It was New Year's Eve and I was astounded that my doctor allowed me to leave the hospital for a few hours to have an early dinner with my family and friends. Approaching the sliding doors to exit, I smiled as I looked up at the brilliant blue sky thinking *here comes the sun*. I took a deep breath, lifted myself out of the wheelchair and stepped outside. I was eager to have a change of scenery. I needed to breathe fresh air, feel the sun against my face and hear the crunching of snow beneath my feet. I could hardly believe I was going to have dinner at Kirin, a phenomenal restaurant in Vancouver. We had three full tables of family that came to celebrate the New Year with us. The smiles and stories reminded me of why I needed to fight. Being surrounded by people I loved poured the meaning of life into me even if the results were merely temporary. When dinner ended, as if I belonged in the custody of the hospital, I was returned to my reality.

The initial shock of my condition wore off and I accepted my fate. Nevertheless, my next stage was anger. *When I allowed my anger to take over, it was the most destructive thing I could have done.*

I wasn't any different. Like countless others, I didn't understand why I developed this illness instead of the pedophile, drug dealer, murderer or someone else that destroyed life. I couldn't escape the thought or comprehend a child having to endure what I found difficult to handle. I wouldn't want them to feel the kind of anger and pain that enveloped me. No child should be afflicted with this disease or any other. No one should!

Exhaustion made it easy not to care. My befuddled mind, drained from the gamut of emotions running through it, would shut down on its own. Existing that way was simply buying time until I died. I had a lot of time to feel sorry for myself because my ability to live the way I wanted was stolen. The irony of my situation is that I wasted the entire year prior to having leukemia without considering my actions. It's disconcerting to reminisce about the things I took for granted and the time I should've been investing into my future. Living to have few regrets is how I should have lived. If I had any idea this was going to be my fate, I wouldn't have made so many mistakes, but it was too late. I decided, since I was going out, I'd go pain-free.

    I was laden with a rancorous cancer causing insufferable and inflammatory pain. My physical changes were unpleasant and continued speeding down an unyielding path. My weight constantly increased and I felt more lethargic than ever. When I'd wake up in the morning, after lifting my head from the pillow, I'd find patches of hair. It had fallen out like pine needles from a dying tree. The first few times it happened, I lost it. Then, I realized, it was a part of the inevitable process. I had to just go with it until it was gone.

    My body craved the pain medications and I allowed it. I kept trying to believe I had a chance at beating the disease but with every handful of pills I swallowed or dose of medication injected into my IV, I found my probability of holding onto hope washing away. Once the pain medications securely claimed their place, it seemed they were the only thing between pain and death. The doctor gave me dilaudid, which was an opioid analgesic for severe pain, as often as needed. The doctors knew the type of pain I was in and they wanted me to be as comfortable as possible. Obviously, I took the liberty of hitting the button that dispersed the dosage of medication like I was answering a question on a game show. The problem was, my body had become used to the medication. When I took the dilaudid it gave me a nice warm rush through my chest, calming me down; it felt good for about two minutes and for the next ten, I felt horrible. The pain became so intense my doctor allowed me to have it every twelve minutes and I took it like clockwork. The dilaudid was highly addictive, but in my case an addiction wasn't the concern, death was.

A day didn't pass where *I couldn't feel the cancer killing me.* Acute lymphoblastic leukemia known as ALL is the most common type of leukemia in young children. This disease affects adults as well and had no problem claiming me. Unfortunately, I fell into a limited range of adults that have or will be affected by this disease. Sadly, it attacks those age sixty-five and older too, and just as quietly as it had me.

My only chance at life was a bone marrow transplant because death was playing its cards well and it had a much better hand than I did. The hospital listed me with the Provincial Bone Marrow Registry and the Canadian Bone Marrow Registry so I had to exercise patience and wait. It was almost one in a million they would find a perfect match in time, but I had no other recourse.

Confinement was inescapable and it didn't look like I'd ever walk out of the hospital. I was too weak to do anything except revisit my life. My thoughts returned to spring break, during my senior year of high school, with Jen.

Chapter 6

Separation Anxiety

In 2000 I was hit with an unforeseen scenario that took a long while to reconcile with me. In a relatively casual conversation, Mum informed us she was going back to England to help care for her grandmother who was ailing in health. I knew Mum missed her family and the type of life she had in England yet, I couldn't fathom her decision to leave us behind.

Once she left, I was absolutely lost because Mum and I were awfully close. Although no one really knew me, she came closer than anyone else.

As the year progressed, Mum's absence became even more challenging for me to accept. I had a deep separation anxiety, which was difficult to manage because I didn't know if what I felt was normal or not. I hadn't anticipated it taking a toll on me and I didn't know how to deal with the negative emotions sprouting. The loneliness I carried continued to dig its hole inside of me a little more profoundly, one month after another. While Dad was going through his normal routine it was hard to believe I was the only one to see something wrong with Mum being gone. I couldn't help but to speculate about the way my father managed the situation. From my viewpoint it didn't look like he was doing too well either.

Finally, spring break rolled around. Jen and I caught a flight to visit Mum in a metropolitan borough in North West England, Manchester. I loved it there because I found it to be one of the gnarliest great cities with an unbelievable history of music spawning numerous British bands in the '80s. I felt free.

All I could think about was spending time with Mum. Before I had the chance to get settled or relish in seeing her I was ignited by a surreal and very nonchalant conversation. Her words caused my calm and exultant core to become completely dark and enraged. As if I should've seen it coming, in her typical British tone reflecting little emotion or sadness, Mum casually informed me she and Dad were divorcing. Without further warning, I plunged into an icy pool of negative emotions, brooding in utter disbelief. They were planning on signing away over twenty years together and completely dismantle our lives along with theirs. Everything with Dad's career, or better yet, in his world seemed to be going well. I didn't think life could've been better for him, but clearly I was wrong. I maintained a much closer relationship with Mum than Dad. The way she communicated something that unexpected, caught me off guard and thrust me into an uncontainable ball of rage. Now *I* was going to become a statistic and if I wanted to see Mum I'd have to travel to the other side of the world. Rage took ahold of me and I responded with a purely emotional discharge of negativity, which caused me to get into a fight with a brick wall. I lost. My parent's decision encouraged me to feel something I didn't know was there. I never thought anything could hurt so badly. I wanted my family to stay exactly the way they were, together. I couldn't see us any other way, nor did I want to. We weren't perfect and I didn't fit, but they were all I had.

When the nurse entered the room I vacated my dejected thoughts and gave her my full attention or as much of it as I could.

Chapter 7

Walking Away From Defeat

With great difficulty, there were occasions I forced myself to feel somewhat normal. It was hard, but I kept trying to find ways to be positive. I grew tired of lying in bed, waiting to die. I thought if I were able to get up and walk around, I'd feel better. I didn't expect to walk down a long corridor but I wanted to try to go a few yards at a time just to take a shower or go to the bathroom. Since I was dying, everything felt like a considerable challenge both mentally and physically and I needed to break free of that.

It took a lot to eat, breathe, move, sit, talk, think and lie to everyone so they'd believe I was stronger and more resilient than I actually was. By the time I did all of that, I didn't have energy for much else. The countdown for a chance at life had nearly faded from my body and memory. With unsteady hands, I'd press my pump for pain medication and let it go to work.

Being in the hospital was very uncomfortable. The temperature in my room stayed cold but there were several occasions I was unusually warm and found it difficult to breathe. Being in the cancer ward for several weeks turned out to be incapacitating, especially since I understood I'd probably never leave there alive.

It was near the end of January and I remember thinking I would've given anything to stand outside in the rain. I envisioned holding my head back, with my arms stretched out wide as I welcomed the opportunity to blend my tears without anyone knowing. I'd release every bit of pain and sorrow by allowing it to roll down my face, drop to the ground and wash away. If the thunder was kind enough to grace me with several loud crashes, I'd discharge the anger inside of me right along with it.

As the weeks passed, my muscles became weaker and I rarely got out of bed. One particular day, I decided I didn't want to lie there and have a sponge bath. I wanted to feel the streams from the shower cover my body, like rain. When I expressed my feelings to the nurse, she allowed it. Cautioning me to be careful, the nurse set the shower temperature, placed everything I needed on the counter and then helped me walk into the bathroom. With slow and careful movements I stepped into the shower. Before I gained complete confidence, my legs felt flimsy like gelatin and within seconds, I crashed helplessly to the floor making a couple of loud thumps. The nurse rushed into the bathroom only to find me lying in the shower, crying loud and hard. Everything I'd been hiding inside of me along with each measure of unbearable pain that had been tucked away was involuntarily discharged.

I don't think Dad ever knew, but during the moments I really lost it or when I was about to, he happened to be my strongest pillar of strength. Dad never caved in by offering negative words of defeat or actions. His persistence in remaining positive was unwavering even if he didn't have a solution. Dad managed to convince me that *this*, meaning everything I had to endure, is what was supposed to happen so I could get better *and I believed him*.

Less than a week later, the longing I had to get out of that hospital bed wouldn't dissipate. It refused to go away with my last failed attempt because the bed started to feel more like a coffin. The constant in and out of the doctors, nurses and aids made it impossible to rest peacefully even when I was exhausted. My routine of pressing the pain medication pump and trying to forget what I was going through, from one hour to the next, is all I really had to do. Besides watching an insane amount of cartoons and comedy shows on television, I drowned myself in music.

I focused on humor because laughter provided temporary relief and became a distraction from the intractable cancer pain. Leukemia waged war with a hateful vengeance and it worked diligently to annihilate my body. Since I didn't have any weapons to fight it, I wanted that war to stay out of my head. The combination of music, comedy and pain medication turned out to be a coping mechanism.

Some days were excruciatingly brutal and the overwhelming emotion causing me to concede to giving up, filtered into my consciousness. Before I went too far with that thought I remembered what my brother Jeremy told me. Jeremy attended Shawnigan Lake in 1995; we graduated together. He and I became good friends and once I got to know him, he became my brother.

The day after Christmas, Jeremy came to the hospital in an effort to keep my spirit light. After one look at me, he instantly understood why I was afraid. I was so drugged up; the person he once knew was barely there. I was overweight and had chemo brain, which meant I couldn't remember much. I attributed my memory loss to the extensive combination of prescribed drugs. Jeremy could see the vacancy in my eyes and feel the emptiness upon my soul as if I'd already checked out. He knew I wanted to surrender. I don't know why, but it wasn't acceptable to him. Jeremy said, *"You just gotta power through this!"*

    I didn't know what he meant at the time, because I didn't have any power, but after weeks of willingly sinking into a deceptive mode of accepting death, I understood. I wasn't fighting or even using everything I had. My contribution of putting in full effort had yet to be made and I knew it. I was tired of doing nothing and allowing cancer to win so I said to myself, "Do something! Fight!" I shook my head and decided *I won't back down*. I alleged doing so would be my way of fighting death. Courageously, every time I felt it push me, I pushed right back at death as hard as I could and kept on fighting. After allowing helplessness to discourage me, I convinced myself I was stronger than I thought.

    I didn't have an alternative besides fighting this illness so determination forced me to take positive steps towards change. Instead of being wheeled down to x-ray the next morning, I decided to walk. Helplessness and defeat were infiltrating my mind like smoke from a raging fire. I needed to remove them before they permanently moved in or suffocated me.

I was up early waiting anxiously for someone to take me to x-ray. When the orderly showed up with a wheelchair ready to go, I rotated myself to the side of the bed and slowly allowed my feet to touch the floor. I was going to walk. While gripping the stainless steel rail on the bed I began to push myself up. Before completely standing, a slight tremble warned me that my muscles weren't strong enough to handle the weight of my body, but I continued. After a few unstable steps, I tripped over my feet and fell down, smashing my knee into the ground. I released a painfully loud and angry moan, which was more about disappointment than anything else. I was used to pain.

It took two nurses along with the attendant to pick me up and place me in the wheelchair where I belonged. The fear I managed to push away over the past few weeks was eager to dive right back into me. I knew if I didn't put forth more effort, I'd remain this way. I failed again and my feelings were bruised, but I was determined to get up and keep trying until I could walk on my own because it's what I wanted. Being confined to a bed had weakened my muscles and I needed to make them stronger. Physical therapy and faith were a good beginning. I would do it.

Psychologically I'd met a temporary defeat, but it wasn't over. While being taken down to the x-ray, I massaged my knee and decided I'd try again later.

I thought about Mum being back in Canada after having been so far away. With complete ease, I slipped back to an earlier time. The orderly continued talking as he pushed me down the long corridor once again, but his voice faded as my memory sailed away.

Chapter 8

Life Has A Path For Everyone

Jen and I returned home to Canada after spring break. Implementing an unflappable exit strategy, Mum appeared to conclude her parental role, leaving Dad to finish the job whether he wanted to or not. She punched out as if deciding she wasn't putting in overtime. Without providing any input, I watched them terminate their marriage. Upon my high school graduation, they were done and that was it. I was certain the cause originated from both parties and perhaps Dad a little more than Mum, although I never knew all of the details. It appeared as if Dad owned an aching sadness, *along with a touch of grey*, something I didn't want to inherit.

For the first few years Mum returned on a consistent basis, but as time passed her visits became less frequent.

It took some time and a lot of effort before I was able to consciously detach myself from Mum. Alleviating our close connection kept me from getting hurt again. I didn't want it with anyone if I didn't have it with her. I'm quite sure the pain she caused wasn't intentional and I knew she had her own, but it still hurt.

I resided in Canada and Mum continued thriving in Europe as if she never had kids. I was secretly devastated. I wasn't the easiest kid to have but I was far from being unworthy of a Mum that I loved more than myself. Her choices made me challenge the validity of the relationship I thought we had up until that point. I needed to protect my volatile emotions because they'd become more than I could handle if I didn't.

When Mum left, she rendered an overwhelmingly harsh blow to my already poor self-esteem and I don't think she realized it. I needed to alter my mentality, accept the emptiness and perhaps remain that way so I wouldn't get sideswiped or hurt again. Other than that, I didn't know what I was supposed to do. My anger was dangerous and painful because it generated an intense feeling of worthlessness. Sometimes, people that feel worthless do desperate things and at times I felt I was nearing that path.

I continued my journey through life carrying, but not dealing with, several of my own issues. Although Dad never asked for it, I dragged a bag of sympathy for him because I felt terrible watching him deal with the divorce. Of course, I knew he wasn't perfect and I don't know anyone who is, but he didn't leave Canada and more importantly, he didn't leave his kids. I had great difficulty releasing the feeling of being abandoned by Mum. Whatever the reason, it shouldn't have taken her out of the country. Mum knew Jen and I were graduating high school and most likely became more at ease since we *were* adults. Admittedly, she had the right to do whatever she needed or even wanted because she was an adult too. I felt Mum behaved as if it were her chance to make a break from life in Ft. McMurray because she was done raising us. Yes, she did a great job, but she was still our Mum and I never really thought of that part coming to an end. In retrospect, I'd always believed she missed her life in England and most of her family was still there. Over the years, I noticed she remained accustomed with the British ways of living. Mum, made the most incredible meals and her dinners reminded me of her rich history and love for it.

Upon graduating from high school, I worked with Dad at his Creeative Woodworking Company during the summer. I liked the name because it embraced the essence of our heritage. Being around Dad made me want to discover a way to utilize my creativity and passion the way he had. Once summer ended, I took the opportunity to learn more about my passion for music and found a way to become a part of it.

I moved to Vancouver to attend school at the Center for Digital Imaging and Sound. I attended the school for a year and began learning the intricacies of music but had difficulty grasping some of the theoretical perspectives and passing tests. My frustrations mounted because I couldn't comprehend how I was able to live and breathe music but not exhale the concepts and nail the tests. I knew more than anyone would've imagined but it wasn't reflected where it needed to be, on paper. I believed that roadblock was going to prohibit me from putting my passion to use the way I desired and I didn't know what else to do. Unsure of my direction and disillusioned with myself, I returned to Ft. McMurray.

There was so much I wanted to achieve but I couldn't seem to break into anything. A career in music is where I belonged and what I sought more than anything else. The thought of failing pressed heavily on my conscious and returned me to my depressing existence. The disappointment was nothing less than agonizing.

I felt like a loser because there was so much pressure to be what my Dad was and I didn't want to do anything he did. No one knew it but if I didn't follow in his footsteps, I wouldn't be compared to him. I wanted to be *his* son but I wasn't *that* son. I wasn't a businessperson and lacked the professional acumen he displayed. He was great with people but I was shy and awkward. In the '90s I wore baggy pants, flannel shirts and had long greasy hair. Dad was sharp and he hated my method of self-expression. Learning the family business with Dad wouldn't work because I was extremely intimidated by my father and his success. I couldn't navigate past it. I always wondered why I was so different from my mother and sister too. I didn't belong anywhere, even though I wanted to. I couldn't manage it for anything. Life took Mum down one path, Dad on another, Jen had hers and I needed to find the right one for me.

Chapter 9

Radiation Treatment

Knowing there were other terminally ill patients throughout the confines of Vancouver General Hospital, I couldn't help but wonder how they were handling their fate. Were they reviewing their mistakes or challenges? Did regrets plague them or had forgiveness relieved them? Were they counting down the hours while staring at the *walls and windows*? Had they surrendered to making peace with their loved ones? Did they wonder what happens next? Had anger consumed them? Were they afraid to die?

Time to deliberate over the finality of my life while lying in bed, adjusting to the unsettling feeling of death, was all I had. After being there for so long, I realized death lives comfortably in a hospital. It's there, waiting to claim one victim after another, devastating families along the way.

How anyone held it together while dealing with a significant or terminal illness remained beyond my comprehension. I was in a place the employees didn't appear to offer more than what their specific job allowed. I didn't perceive there to be much of a human factor present either. Instead, I watched a meticulous and calculated daily routine transpire with little communication or expression of sympathy. It appeared as if the staff were discouraged from becoming attached to the patients, especially in my ward. Perhaps, the high turnover had the ability to cause their emotional ramifications to be far too traumatic.

When you remain confined to a room for as long as I'd been, it's surprising what I noticed. The number of ceiling tiles, the pattern of my heart monitor, scuffs on the walls and little details that are predominantly overlooked, now captured my attention. Hanging on the wall directly in front of my bed was a white, dry eraser board. Every time my blood was checked the nurse wrote the numbers on it. I saw my count becoming worse and encountered a horrible feeling of defeat knocking again. I didn't want it, so I tried to convince myself I could make my blood count better. When I put the thought of getting better in the front of my mind, it seemed as though I did. At times my numbers went up just a little bit, but at least they went up.

My body underwent both radiation and chemotherapy at the same time because the vicious war inside of me was raging out of control. The chemo and rounds of radiation were fighting a disease promising to kill me. Sadly, the aftermath of that war continued to leave additional physical and emotional threats. Sometimes, the pain became so bad I curled up into a ball because the slightest bit of movement was intolerable. Since I had trouble making it from the hospital bed to the shower without falling, my effort to gain mobility had diminished over time. The first time I'd fallen caused me to bruise like someone had beaten me with a hockey stick. After that, walking became increasingly difficult. I'm sure the continuum of weight gain caused by the prednisone didn't help.

After beginning the chemo treatments it proved to be difficult just going to the radiation room, and I wasn't walking. I didn't want to be moved because of the nausea or touched due to the pain.

Having radiation was the easiest procedure I underwent because it was painless. However, it was the most detrimental since there were high-powered beams of radiation infiltrating my body that left my skin red, dry and feeling sunburned. The purpose of this treatment was to damage the leukemia cells in my body in an attempt to stop their out of control growth. The disheartening part of it all was the effects made me feel like I was fighting a battle I'd eventually lose. Being submerged in hopelessness became my penalty. Most of the time, I'd put on my headphones, hit the pain pump and close my eyes until it was time for some kind of treatment or test.

The hospital had a lot of uncomfortable places but the one I disliked the most was the radiation room. It was a scary place. Adjusting to being in that room, regardless of how many times I'd been, was stressful.

In the center of the room there was a bed placed securely on the floor. Since the machine was old and I was rather tall, the doctors didn't know if it was going to work properly on me. The technician shifted me into an awkward position so my body could fit on the little bed. It was imperative for the passes of radiation to go completely across my entire body to be effective. Leukemia is more prevalent in children, so that machine was manufactured to suit them.

In the first position, I'd lie on my back and stare at the ceiling to find a beach scene and several stickers of Disney characters on the light fixtures. They were probably there as a distraction for every one of the children that laid on that bed begging for a miracle. I wondered how many little eyes had stared at them in a desperate attempt to forget what they were going through. It worked for me. I remember staring at the ceiling, realizing I wasn't feeling any pain.

I couldn't fully understand how something as simple as a light had the ability to kill my diseased cells; nevertheless I became hopeful of the possibility that it could work.

The oddest selection of music played in the background, which added atmosphere to the action taking place. They may have thought it to be calming but I found it downright eerie and unnerving. It sounded like the scene in a horror movie when the music becomes really intense and everyone's watching to see what's going to happen next. Well, perhaps the music was fitting for the doctors since they were waiting for the outcome. To make it worse, when I glanced over to my left, I noticed the doctor, the technician and my parents staring at me through the large window.

The sight of the radiation machine was already unnerving. When I thought about the high beams of radiation attempting to kill something inside of me, it created a truly uncomfortable experience.

When the treatment began, I'd watch the light pass over me. All I could think was, *the good cells are attacking the bad cells*. I'd recite those eight words over and over in my head making sure I believed it was working. On the exterior, I carried myself like Mum would but internally, I was freaking out.

I didn't know much about the radiation treatment except it wasn't a good thing. I had six powerful rounds of radiation in three days and I was given forty passes over my front and forty over my backside twice a day. The amount was tremendous in itself but my body needed more help so they prescribed a very powerful medication called methotrexate.

Methotrexate was another cancer fighting agent that felt like I had pure sulfuric acid poured down my throat. After taking that medication I had to wear an ice necklace wrapped around my neck for twelve days to keep it from swelling. Little slivers of ice chips were all I could manage to slip in between my parched lips. I couldn't eat solid food for weeks and was fed intravenously. That particular medication was *the worst*. It left me with the impression they were doing whatever they could to save my life and that was an extremely desperate attempt.

Methotrexate reminded me of my parent's divorce; it burned and I didn't want it.

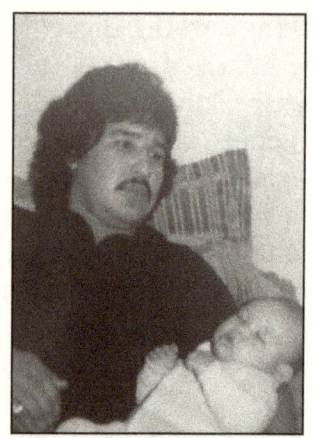
Me as an infant in Dad's arms.

Dad and I at my graduation.

My sister, Jen, and I.

Me, Mom, Jen and Dad.
Shawnigan Lake graduation, June 28, 2000.

A tranquil moment on the water with Dad.

Dad and I fishing.

Me in my element.

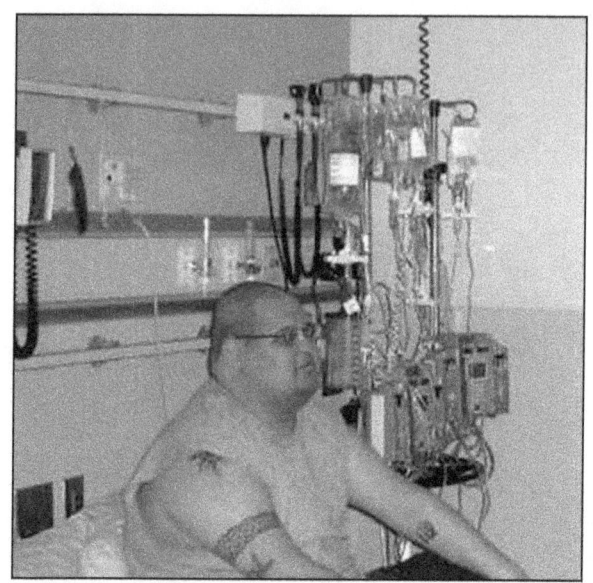

The day of my bone marrow transplant.

Meeting my bone marrow donor for the first time, in 2011.

Chapter 10

A Time For Healing

A little over a year, after my parent's divorce, I decided I'd return to Manchester and spend time with Mum. I was a bit of a mess and it came from carrying around the anger of their divorce. Ironically, it didn't seem to be hurting anyone the way it had me. Dad moved on with his life and Mum had done the same so I thought I'd try to regain what I'd lost and let go of *their past*. I needed to heal.

I moved to Manchester on September 13, 2001 two days after the horrendous tragedy of 9/11. The airport was jammed packed and it took eight hours to get through security, flying out of Calgary. Several flights intended for the U.S. came through Canada. It was the first day flights opened up since 9/11. My flight was booked prior to the tragedy. Having the experience of living abroad was invaluable and I was working on removing fear, so I took the flight.

While sitting on the plane, I couldn't help but to think about the significant loss of life that occurred. I thought about the tremendous degree of hate it took to do such cowardly acts and I wanted nothing but healing for the people of the United States. I needed to let go of my anger and succumb to my own healing with Mum. Our time here is unpredictable making each moment a precious gift not to be squandered. We often forget about those little moments as if they're too insignificant to count, like a penny lying on the ground.

It didn't take much effort before Mum and I were best friends again. Just looking at her striking and elegant features reminded me of how natural her beauty was. As I studied her emerald eyes she seemed to be more at peace and free. Perhaps Manchester was what she needed. It felt great being reunited with Mum because she was exactly what I needed.

Mum owned a beauty salon in Manchester. While she was working, I was anxious to venture out and explore, but as soon as she came home we'd take off to indulge in the magnificence of the city. There were random days she'd designate time entirely to me by taking off instead of going into her salon. She took me to some of the cool places she frequented as a kid and shared what she enjoyed most about the city since moving back. I loved being able to see pieces of her history and appreciated the fervent way she revealed it. Time provided the opportunity for us to heal our relationship as mother and son. The healing may have been more on my part but it happened. The many places we visited, meals we shared and laughter that followed brought us right back to where we belonged. I couldn't help but to have an amazing time. Being with Mum rejuvenated my soul and made me feel alive again.

A dam, filled with unrestrained intensity, ruptured inside of me as I learned more about the history of music that Manchester owned. I couldn't contain my excitement or interest in wanting to know more. The range of music was incredible and included everything from electronic dance music, acid house, techno to rave and more. The Northern Soul scene of the '60s influenced the massive rave scene, which fascinated me to no end. Paired with the impeccable history with the world-renowned Hacienda nightclub and Manchester was the place that enveloped the essence of who I am. I was surrounded by not only music, but also the rich history of it.

The people I encountered had an invigorating candor about them that left me with a lingering curiosity. They seemed to be comfortable with whom they were, which was something I had yet to embrace. Their light-heartedness and genuine sense of being caused me to enjoy the city even more. It wasn't the same in Ft. McMurray; I couldn't find my reflection.

I preserved an insatiable appetite for a big city environment, rich in history, architecture and music. I loved the food, trains and the double-decker buses. Everything about Manchester seemed flawless.

I spent nearly two years with Mum and my time with her was better than imagined. I'm glad I made an effort to get our connection back since *I* was the one that let it dissolve after she left Ft. McMurray. Although Manchester brought some degree of healing I felt I was missing out on a lot and wanted to return to Ft. McMurray. I missed Dad, Jen, the rest of my family and friends. Mum was sad to see me leave while she happy we had time together. Inherently, I needed to return to Canada, which caused me to understand why Mum returned to England.

Before I departed England, I decided to go backpacking with friends and experience more of life in a free-spirited kind of way. I had a really cool faded army green backpack I purchased in Canada so I loaded it with the essentials and took off.

For the first time, I was wide-open to feeling alive and experiencing diverse cultures, food, music and everything life could show me. I couldn't sufficiently explain why the feeling was so intense but life was relentlessly calling me out there. In an overwhelming way, I wanted to take in as much of it as possible. I couldn't wait to venture out into a headwind like an eagle, soaring in solitude.

My journey commenced in Liverpool with an awesome group of friends and from there we ventured off to Amsterdam. Amsterdam had its place in history for art as it inspired the talents of Rembrandt and van Gogh while offering the live version of their inspiration in a panoramic view. The picturesque canals, museums, breathtaking 17th century architecture and cosmopolitan environment were overflowing. I noticed the abundance of pedal bikes and interestingly enough, lack of cars. In fact, it happened to be one of the bikes that almost ran me down.

After departing from our small group of friends, Karsten and I headed to Stuggart, in southwest Germany where the flowers, windmills and greenery captivated my senses in an unbelievable manner. The people were extremely hospitable. I found it quite reminiscent of a major city with authentic restaurants for all types of ethnicities, rich in history and culture. It was surrounded by one of Germany's largest wine growing regions.

My friend's father ran a beautiful five-star hotel just outside of Stuggart, so we stayed there. When I woke up in the morning a delectable banquet of food was waiting downstairs. There were fresh meats, pastries, breads, cheeses, cereal and more. Anything I'd want was right in front of me. We sat down and indulged without hesitation.

After enjoying Stuggart, for a few days we took a comfortable bullet train to Switzerland, stopping in Bern. Giving a slight upward tilt of my nose I inhaled a deep breath of fresh air in absolute disbelief. My eyes widened upon meeting the magnificent mountains surrounding us. Bern was the gateway to the Alps, which was sculpted to absolute perfection.

Our next stop took us to one of the worlds fashion capitals, Milan, Italy. We happened to arrive amidst the pandemonium of fashion week to a potpourri of styles, colors and people from all over the world. Although our visit was brief it was remarkable to take in the unyielding torrent of excitement. After hanging out in the city and enjoying the collection of unique fashions, an eclectic mix of trends, incredible Italian cuisine and unique culture, we returned to the station to catch the first train out. Our next adventurous destination planned was Nice, France.

Nice had a peaceful and relaxing atmosphere that welcomed us. We stayed in a really cool hostel with a bakery right below it. Intentionally invading my senses, the brisk morning air carried the fresh smell of pastries in through the open window. Unable to resist, I got dressed and promptly headed downstairs to indulge in the bakery's most appetizing pastries.

Exploring Nice meant taking in an enormous palette of pastel colors skillfully painted around the city. Appearing to have been sketched by an artist, entrancingly lining the coast was the extraordinarily rich blue-green Mediterranean Sea. Nice was a compilation of everything from clubs and cafés to eateries and incredible art. It was the perfect place to be that spring.

After a transitory stay in Nice, my friend Karsten returned home and I headed to meet Mum at her second home in Málaga, Spain to conclude an incredible life-changing journey. My mind took in more than it could manage and I felt like a different person. I needed the conversion of negative to positive energy flowing generously inside my body. It made me feel like I was among the living.

A week later, I flew back to Manchester with Mum to spend a few more weeks with her before returning home in April. I couldn't comprehend why I was privileged to take in all of the breathtaking magnificence displayed in the form of untainted inspiration. But I do know it brought about an immediate appreciation to my life. For reasons unknown, we may experience things thought unimaginable and it's meant to be valued and savored, as there is more of life to touch before we leave it. Being mindful of what is out there can help us determine who we are. Although it was time, I didn't want to let go. I was living *above the clouds*.

Chapter 11

The Suffering It Brings

While my oncologist prepared us to accept my inescapable death, over a month had passed and I was still alive. The intense treatments and numerous medications bought a handful of time but I remained frustrated. Knowing, but not having any idea of how much time I had left was difficult to cope with. I couldn't make plans because I didn't know if I'd be able to keep them. I wouldn't say goodbye because I didn't want to do it again and again, like I was eager to die. And I never looked into the future because *I* wasn't there. I had to live in the moment, in that day, from one hour to the next and the psychological ramifications were simply unreal.

I already defied the doctor's original timeline, which gave me hope and a reason to continue fighting. It may not seem possible to fight while lying in bed, waiting to see if the treatments work, but it is. My mind was still capable of telling my body I wanted to live. I was tired, yet I hadn't given up, even when I thought I should. It was difficult to watch my family suffer along with me. I couldn't tell them not to worry because they loved me.

Each day brought visitors, tests, tears, pain and so forth but one of the things that hurt me a great deal was observing what this did to my sister. It was heartbreaking. I tried not to say anything because I couldn't change the situation. There was literally nothing I could do to stop any of this, let alone everyone's pain. But Jen, she should've been having fun in her own life instead of being tormented inside mine. Cancer is something that takes full control of everyone's emotional state until it's done; even then, its deadly toxins linger. I couldn't tolerate my family or loved ones experiencing any of this. They didn't realize that I felt their pain and recognized the tireless effort they made to hide it

Mum stayed with me quite a bit and Dad equally so, but when they left along with everyone else, I thought about my two enemies, *time* and *cancer*. Each morning presented the personal agony of knowing the foreseeable consequences while waiting for a donor. Even if I had one my doctors weren't certain the transplant would take. I pushed the thought of time to the back of my mind and impatiently waited while cancer silently continued its destructive reign.

After doing an initial search, my physician informed me, as of yet, there weren't any donor matches. Instead of giving up, she added me to the World Bone Marrow Data Registry, hopeful something would manifest. This was their final effort to save my life because if I didn't get one, all hope for a chance to live would vanish. Waiting, was nothing short of an intense nightmare. I was petrified some days and numb on the others. Still, I did my best to keep it hidden since I was good at it.

I had to exercise patience, *be positive* about the search and wait. The other choice was, give up and die. The sparks of humor and optimism I held onto slipped between my fingers like melting snow. Since the doctor remained pessimistic, I considered being more accepting of that one-way ticket out of here. The leukemia remained aggressive in its attack and I had difficulty thinking about the damage; so I tried to shut that part out of my mind.

My chemo treatments occurred daily and were done intravenously. It seemed strange because the chemo hadn't affected me too much until I began my second intense round of treatments. Keeping anything down was nearly impossible while the pain was absolutely *bad to the bone!* There wasn't one particular type of pain because *everything* hurt and all the time.

In February 2007, the doctors realized I didn't have a donor and they couldn't do anymore than what they were already doing. After being warned about my frailty and advised to be cautious around anyone that was sick, they released me to go home. In actuality, what they were doing was allowing me to go home and die with dignity, surrounded by my family, friends and the things I loved most. I never anticipated I'd go home, especially after my initial prognosis and rapid decline thereafter, but I didn't expect to be alive either. My doctor made it clear the chemotherapy wasn't over. I had to return to Vancouver General Hospital daily for continued treatments. Grabbing at the ability to feel slightly normal again was a thought I couldn't fathom being within my reach. Now that it was in front of me I took it for however long I'd have.

Dad went out of his way to make everything as convenient for me as possible. He rented an apartment in downtown Vancouver so I'd be close to the hospital for not only my treatments, but in case of an emergency. Without hesitation, the Tuccaro family pulled together to help in any way necessary. As for Dad, he felt more like a father during this crisis than any other period in my life. I was grateful to have everyone's support in the capacity I did because I couldn't imagine what loneliness and difficulties I would've encountered otherwise. Dad, Mum, Jen, other family members and close friends pitched in, making sure I didn't need to ask for anything. It was humbling and inspiring at the same time. They seemed to instinctively be there; making sure I never felt I had to withstand this alone, and I didn't.

Sleeping in wasn't an option irrespective of how I felt on any given day. Regardless of how fatigued I was; I had to prepare for an eight to twelve hour treatment if I wanted to continue the fight for my life.

Once I was home for a few weeks, I realized the hospital had its advantages. There were numerous periods I vacillated between positive and negative emotions. I believed the influx of pain medications contributed heavily to my negativity and turned into an addiction, impossible to manage on my own. It became more of a struggle for me to let go of my reality. I had to be present every single day, which became unbearable. Initially, I hadn't fully committed because I was immersed with negative thoughts of death that privately consumed me. I had to step away from that destructive mindset and pretend the cancer wasn't eating away at my body even when I could feel it.

Being present meant being a willing participant in my own life by having a positive mental attitude and doing everything required of me, as directed. I had to *want* to live and *believe* I would even when the drugs were convincing me to accept defeat. I had to teach my mind to think of nothing but *life* and hold onto everything that encouraged it, like family.

The chemo, radiation and compilation of drugs that I needed to take daily caused considerable deterioration to my body. The consequences were unquestionable.

I developed avascular necrosis, which is the death of bone tissue due to a lack of blood supply. It led to tiny breaks in my bones that eventually would cause my bones to collapse.

Additionally, I managed to have kidney disease and was speeding towards a regular routine of dialysis.

Being in a hospital bed was one thing, but now my once typical routine became physically challenging. The nausea wasn't as bad as expected, but it was a random inconvenience. Another excruciating issue was the degenerative muscles that caused atrophy. My left leg seemed to be affected the most. Being at home meant there were times I had to walk to the bathroom and out to the car for treatment so I needed to push myself to overcome the challenge of atrophy and get up. One morning I got out of bed and when I tried to stand, my legs fell flaccid and I hit the floor like I fell out of the sky. My degenerating muscles couldn't support my heavy frame and my legs were useless; they were just there. Since I spent most of my time either lying down or sitting up, my muscles became extremely weak. As soon as I made an attempt to stand, the spasms kicked in and I couldn't do anything but scream. The relentless pain consumed me as my cries echoed into the air until it gradually subsided. There wasn't anything anyone could do to stop it.

While I had no desire to spend half of each day in the hospital, giving consideration to deviating from my regiment wasn't feasible. It encompassed a stringent routine I had to follow without opposition. Regardless of how medicated I was, I knew that much. No one had time to fight or beg me to live, nor should they have to. This was my life and my fight.

When morning came, it was difficult to get up because my nights were filled with restlessness and heavy sweats. By the time my feet needed to hit the floor the thought alone turned menacing. I moved about carefully to avoid bumping into anything so I wouldn't bruise myself.

When I looked in the mirror, the reflection looking back wasn't me. It was pale and lifeless. His weight was heavier than the two hundred and seventy-five pounds I typically maintained. Thanks to the prednisone and inability to exercise, the guy in the mirror was three hundred and eighty-five pounds and unrecognizable to my eyes.

Chemotherapy began at seven each morning regardless of how I felt. Everything I ate was generally bland since my stomach was particularly sensitive and I didn't want to remain in a constant state of nausea. After getting ready, I'd grab a bowl of cereal, a piece of fruit or a couple pieces of toast before lethargically heading out into the cold. I left my apartment by six-thirty.

Each day brought the same monotonous routine and I was forced to roll with it. Frigid air owned the day, drugs ran through my veins and fear possessed my heart. I hit a point where I wanted everything to stop. I was exhausted from trying, hoping and waiting for something to change as I watched leukemia ripping apart everyone that cared about me. I just wanted all of it to end but I didn't know how. Completely overrun with frustration, I got dressed and shoved my true feelings into that cavernous hole inside of me and waited for Dad with an impetuous grin.

As usual, Dad arrived promptly to take me to the hospital. It was strange, but I could tell that day wasn't going to be like the others. Much like Mum, Dad was attentive to every detail of my health care and made it a point to stay involved irrespective of the obligations he had to his companies. I actually felt like I was his priority.

Until this point, I thought I'd managed to elude the constant, around-the-clock nausea the second round of chemo promised to bring. I assumed I'd been through the worst part of the treatments and looked forward to having some kind of merciful break but that morning began with a few cautionary signs. I felt sick before breakfast and suffered a severe migraine. As usual, I kept breakfast pretty simple having a bowl of cheerios with soymilk, a banana and a piece of dry toast.

Immediately after we got in the car and headed to the hospital I broke out into a cold sweat and started shaking. It didn't take but a few minutes before I became very lightheaded and then nauseous. Right before the Burrard St. Bridge in Vancouver, I warned Dad I was going to be sick. He quickly pulled the car over to the side of the road and I swung open my door just in time. The disgusting combination of toxic medicines penetrated the inside of my mouth reminding me I wasn't getting any better. I was a complete mess.

I crossed over to the worse side of chemo and found I had to stay close to a bathroom, which created tight boundaries. The dry heaves that went along with the persistent vomiting made it worse. When the pain hit, I couldn't curl up tight enough to make it stop. My headaches from the chemo were like having a migraine on steroids. I constantly felt like a massive ball of pain and would've given anything for all of it to stop.

We made it to my appointment and somehow I was still intact until I had to lie on a table for the procedure. They took a long drill and stuck it into my back trying to get the spinal fluid to force the chemo up my spine. Dad laid across another table only a couple feet from me trying to divert my attention away from the buzzing sound of the drill. He knew I couldn't take anymore poking and prodding, except it was an unavoidable part of my care. I envisioned my face turning a shade of crimson reflecting terror and pain, but so had Dad's.

Even though I thought I'd become used to feeling the ongoing deterioration of my body, I hadn't. My new symptoms were overly dramatic. The random muscles spasms continued, increasing in severity throughout my body as desired. They were so merciless that I released the loudest, most agonizing screams possible every time they hit. I wondered what my neighbors thought when they heard them. The pain in my bones and everywhere else remained excruciating but I had to take it because pain was my constant companion.

Whether it was early in the morning or the middle of the night, medicating myself with pain pills was the only thing I could do to try and dull the pain or sleep. Quite honestly, medicating myself as much as possible was the only way I could exist and I became accustomed to the invited state of numbness it provided. I don't think anyone noticed or really cared how many of the painkillers I had in my system. My nightstand, and countertops were covered with orange prescription bottles and it seemed like I took them around-the-clock.

I don't think anyone really considered I was an addict since it wouldn't have mattered if I were; I was dying. The pain and prescriptions from my doctor cancelled that label. I needed them, but not solely for the reasons anyone would've thought. Everything was too much for me and it had been for several lonely years. The leukemia just caused the collapse.

It began in high school and slowly amassed with my inability to fit in. The feeling of inadequacy is something I carried daily and it evolved when I failed at nearly everything I tried to accomplish. I realized I could never be my father and knowing the disappointment I must have caused him was crushing. When Mum left, the loneliness from her absence was something I didn't handle too well. She was my inspiration and somehow always managed to lift me up and send me on my way to try it again. At that time, she didn't make me feel like I wasn't good enough. After she left, I fell into the stage of feeling victimized and everything descended from there. For several years, I remained an emotional mess. When I approached twenty-four, I gave into temptation and the beginning of self-destruction. I tried to conceal my pain with drugs because I didn't understand what I was feeling.

It isn't worth carrying pain, let alone someone else's. Every negative situation from my past needed to stay there. I should've courageously walked away and gone into my future ready to embrace life with more wisdom and knowledge *just like Dad*. When things happened I was supposed to take the lesson and leave the pain behind where it belonged. Instead, I made the mistake of taking every destructive experience and emotion with me. Because I was hurting didn't mean whomever caused it was too. Most likely, they'd gone on with their life not having any inclination of their negative imprint on me. I hadn't learned to let go and that alone was a detriment.

Part of the problem was the way I chose to handle situations in my life. I couldn't blame anyone for my journey because it was mine, along with all of the choices in it. Consequently, I allowed it to affect me.

A year and a half later, the painkillers had become necessary in order for me to look like I was able to function because I couldn't on my own. After awhile, most of my days were spent in a dense fog. I found it pathetic that rather than talking about my problems or seeking help, I chose to keep them to myself. I handled what little fragment of life I had left quietly and destructively with drugs, and they matched my personality perfectly. Drugs masked the pain and avoided addressing the real problems. When they wore off, both were still very real and present.

Before I commenced with chemotherapy and radiation treatments my blood cell count was extremely low in essential components. After the treatments I had more of a decrease in my cell count, which was the reason I needed to have blood transfusions. Although extremely intense therapy was killing the leukemia or lymphoma cells in my marrow, it was killing blood producing stem cells as well. There were times when a part of my treatment included having a blood transfusion, but ultimately I needed several. The platelets I received came in a thick plastic bag and resembled orange juice. When I needed platelets, they hooked me up to the machine and gave me a transfusion.

Seven days a week, I was hooked up to my IV and had chemo for several hours. When I sat back in my chair and let the process take place, it was really hard to watch other patients undergoing chemo. From one day to the next, I saw women, men, mothers, fathers, grandparents and far too many little children just beginning their life. I saw it and it made me cringe. *Cancer has an ugly reality to it. It's a vile and selfish disease that doesn't discriminate*; it doesn't care who it takes or the damage it leaves behind.

It would seem I should be used to the pain because I've suffered through deep-seated layers of it physically, emotionally and mentally. I'd been stuck with more needles than most would imagine. I sat still time after time to have a drill and then long needle delicately inserted into my spine. I lost my hair when I had radiation treatment and looked like I fell asleep in the blazing sun. I couldn't walk on my own, shower or use the facilities without help. When the spasms came, I'd practice clearing my lungs. I've spent as much time in the hospital as I did at home during my outpatient treatment sometimes forgetting where I was supposed to stay. When my illness showed signs of getting bad, they'd keep me as a precaution. Regardless, it was still my job to show up and contribute to saving my life with an unfaltering positive attitude. When I lost it, I had to glue myself back together and continue on. All of it was a part of my battle so I had to take it just like the others.

I alleged *my seasons in the abyss* were upon me. I'd been dying for months and nearly every crevice of my being had been filled with profound darkness. I became so used to the drugs being in my system I didn't want to function without them. The disease feasted on my body, triggering more pain, threatening my life and leaving me in a constant drug induced state of being high. My will to live came into question again. I pushed through the process and tried to fight with everything I had. What I felt was tremendous guilt over my family. The problem was, they'd been fighting along with me since the day of my diagnosis and I didn't want to let them down. I couldn't properly articulate what I was going through and how much destruction I'd endured because my physical state hadn't improved.

Complaining about the same thing has the ability to sound redundant. There's only so many ways to describe pain and once you've done it there's not much else to say, even when it gets worse. I'd been holding everything inside for such a long time I didn't think my best effort was working any longer.

I stretched out on my sofa, fluffed the pillow behind my head and the door to my memories reopened; Dad stepped through first.

Chapter 12

A Quest To Find My Passion

Upon returning home to Canada, I only had a few days before taking off again. Dad traveled a lot, often inviting Jen and I to go with him. This time, he took us to New York and then Boston. Boston delivered an opportunity for me to observe my father in an arena I wasn't familiar with. His history was far more impressive than I'd ever known. It wasn't until I saw Dad take the podium to speak, that I became filled with inspiration. An overwhelming sense of admiration inundated me for several reasons. I knew a lot about Dad but there were numerous achievements he accomplished without having an audience. I didn't fully grasp the magnitude of his success or the numerous sacrifices he made. His journey encountered challenges many wouldn't have the patience or discipline to overcome. My father didn't brag about his endeavors, he simply got them done. He remained a quiet force, which was a rich character trait of his.

Once he confidently took to the podium at Harvard University and began sharing his narrative as an aboriginal businessman, I realized I didn't know much about my father. I thought I retained a solid comprehension of Dad's business expertise until I heard his story as a member of the audience. Listening to his speech was a pinnacle part of learning more about his accomplishments and reasons for them. Family motivated Dad. His remarkable account of overcoming obstacles was emotionally stirring, yet purely inspirational.

In his twenties, Dad worked diligently as a heavy equipment operator in the oil sands and used part of his income to purchase a taxi license in Ft. McMurray. Decades later, he negotiated with the oil-sands chief executives on contracts for everything from heavy hauling to laboratory services.

As a minority, Dad experienced a tremendous amount of negativity but remained determined not to give in or give up. He made the decision to overcome it, to avoid becoming a victim. Dad's speech was well received. Harvard embraced my father, our culture and his successful history. It was an honor to witness such an empowering presentation. I was extraordinarily proud of my father and radiated with unprecedented pride. *I* needed to figure out what to do with my life.

Europe provided me with a phenomenal release of negativity and delivered a dose of much needed encouragement. Experiencing life in another country at twenty-one, was a remarkable opportunity. It helped me realize that my unfounded insecurities kept me from accepting challenges and progressing. Somehow, I needed to change the way I viewed myself. I had plenty of time to live without judgment or criticism in Europe, which made me feel stronger. I let go, ventured out in the best way imaginable and discovered that life was good! Learning more about Dad injected me with the synergy, direction and passion I'd been looking for. I want to try again.

Jen and I discussed my interest in fashion since I determined it was time to explore the creative side of it. I clung to the insatiable urge to do something I could be proud of. Instinctively, I'd always been drawn to the artistic process of certain things such as music and fashion. Finding an outlet for my uniqueness along with my appetite for self-expression was crucial to making me feel I owned some degree of value. I decided to begin by soliciting a graffiti artist to design colorful t-shirts to demonstrate my ingenuity. My friend Karsten was naturally talented so I asked him to design an awesome prototype.

After sharing my plethora of ideas with Jen, she expressed a genuine interest in the concept. Her support was rather encouraging and logically, I was concerned with Dad's perspective. I was hoping to gain his approval.

I was particularly uneasy at the thought of having to tell a tough, rugged and athletic father like mine that I wanted to attend fashion school, but I did. I gathered my ideas together and gave him a verbal proposal. I don't know why I was worried about telling Dad because he supported it without any reservation. Dad was encouraging in regards to the majority of initiatives I presented. I think it bothered him to observe me wandering through life, wasting time without accomplishing anything. He wanted me to discover my passion and find myself as badly as I did. If I didn't, it wouldn't be for lack of trying.

When we returned to Canada I began inquiring into schools. Julian Casablanca was the lead singer of the American rock band called, The Strokes. While in Manchester I attended a concert on their first tour and loved the band. As I commenced searching for schools, the John Casablanca's Institute was taken under consideration. Ultimately it became my choice.

By the time autumn zestfully emerged in 2002 I'd rented an apartment in Vancouver close to the Institute. I chose it because their educational platform was targeted more towards business, which is what I needed to learn. Eager to interpret my passion from the inside, I retained everything like upsalite. I sought to have something of my own and thought it would make Dad proud of me. Besides, I wanted to be proud of myself.

Once again, the problem wasn't my passion or focus, but that I tested poorly. Humiliation swept across my face and plunged into the depths of my soul. Having a reminder of the academic struggles I encountered at Shawnigan Lake made me feel incapable of achieving my goals. No one really understood how badly I needed to experience some measure of success for my own psychological benefit because *I tried*. When I couldn't make it happen, I felt like a failure, yet again. Regardless of how hard I applied myself the results weren't reflected in my grades. Since I had trouble testing well enough to pass, it didn't look like I'd be able to earn my degree. I felt like I was wasting Dad's money. Disillusioned with life and extremely lost, when I left school, I left that passion.

Void of creative options, I returned to Ft. McMurray and started off in management at one of Dad's companies. I appreciated that the opportunity was always there, but it wasn't right for me. I went to work, did what I had to do and headed home after my shift. I was passed around from one company to another and worked wherever they needed help. Sometimes they sent me to the lower ranks of the company to perform manual labor. It didn't matter; I cleaned and then filled the large bottles that went on top of the water cooler just like the others. The job was physically demanding, but at least I believed I was doing my best, working in that position over the others. Since I developed a real connection with the people, that position became more gratifying. I respected how hard they worked to help make Dad's companies operate productively. Everyone did, but the laboring was tough and I preferred that part of the job.

I injured myself twice so they moved me into management with Neegan Technical Services. Dad provided me with a tremendous opportunity to learn his business in a decision-making capacity, but my interest just seemed to fizzle. I couldn't distinguish how to accomplish what Dad had so effectively done, and I didn't want to be compared to him. I needed to implement my passion and find my purpose in life, so I left.

I had a healthy income working for Dad, but it bothered me I wasn't doing anything to represent my passion or even me. Eager to work in music, I applied for a job at a record shop in town. The crazy part of it was I wanted to be around music so badly; I offered to work without being paid. The owner and manager of the record shop understood my extreme obsession for music and offered me the job at minimum wage. I explained how I wanted to connect people to a more diverse selection of music and give them something they weren't used to, but would appreciate. It didn't take long before management allowed me to order music for the store.

I cultivated my knowledge of music since childhood, causing it to become extensive. Noticing their serious deficiency in hip-hop, I added the necessities along with a few favorites. Cautiously assessing their degree of comprehension and comfort by working my way through the selections, I made sure not to overstep my boundaries. However, I couldn't imagine a record shop that didn't have a killer metal and rock selection. To add a touch of class, I stocked an impressive collection of vinyl records. Vinyl had something that captured the essence of music. Once pressed, in my world it became an artifact.

I was surrounded by music and loved it. I used my passion for music to educate others, but for some reason, fulfillment never came. I stayed there for about three months and once again, I set myself free. I hadn't found myself. I needed to accomplish at least that much before time escaped me.

Chapter 13

Be Positive

The months gradually disappeared leaving an ominous cloud over my befuddled mind. It may have been the drugs or perhaps the fear of fate pressing heavily on my life. Waiting for a bone marrow donor was like expecting nothing because I didn't believe they'd actually find one. I followed the regimen of going through the lethargic motions of each uneventful day feeling the magnetic pull of death.

I spent a lot of time reflecting on various aspects of my life, assessing relationships, replaying the experience of backpacking freely through parts of Europe, and my travels with Dad. I thought about my relationship with Jen and the time we spent at Shawnigan Lake. I could see the vibrancy in her warm smile, I experienced her joy when she laughed and felt her abrupt sadness when I was diagnosed. I agonized over the pain Mum internalized. She barely managed to conceal it beneath her surface. Mum had a few vulnerable moments that slowly escaped like steam. It was difficult to watch her knowing she was holding everything inside. Helpless, wasn't a word that resonated with Mum until cancer entered my life. She'd always been lucid with her thoughts and now she hid them. I wondered how much more she could withstand. It's true that you find out who your friends are in the midst of adversity because I did. Everyone I considered a friend, stood by me in the most admirable way. I couldn't ask for anything else.

I thought about the way I lived, the choices I'd made and every one of my regrets. I wished I could rewind time, but I couldn't. I wanted to tell Mum I was sorry for my anger towards her but she'd already felt it. I never stopped loving Mum. I just needed her. She deserved to live the same way she wanted me to. I should've tried harder not to disappoint my father so many times and put forth more effort because I knew he only wanted the best for me, but now it was too late.

No one can erase or change history. Instead of having regrets, carrying anger or clinging to pain, let it go and live while you can. Like countless others, none of us predicted cancer would decide to wage war against me. We can't predict the future or modify the past, but we can live for the glory as it happens. I spent over four months waiting for the end and while it was taunting, it brought clarity. I spent the time I had to reflect on my life, which meant facing my demons as well.

Out of desperation, I used every scrap of strength, to hold onto whatever inspiration I could find until time caused my sweaty hands to lose their grip. I tried to sustain the illusion of my ability to handle what was happening to me however; my body was failing more rapidly than expressed. There were too many things I could no longer do for myself or even manage without help. This wasn't living and I'd run out of every way to manage doing so.

Regrettably, the psychological imprisonment I kept to myself proved destructive. I'd always hidden from the world and for months, doctors were routinely sifting around inside of me trying to kill the disease living there. I hoped they would discover where it came from. I wanted them to unearth a cure and keep anyone else from the tremendous agony and vile destruction those of us suffered. I had a disease inflicting thousands of unsuspecting people each year. The symptoms were there; all of them. I ignored every single one until it turned catastrophic. I disregarded the warning signs of leukemia because I didn't know what they were.

I clung to life even as death slashed into me causing my hands to bleed profusely. I held on for my family, if nothing else. After several months of treatment, it became impossible for me to hope, dream or believe while dying at the same time.

Since moving into the apartment my state of mind and physical condition deteriorated more rapidly. One afternoon, Dad came over just to get me out of my apartment and depressed frame of mind. I wasn't sure I could handle being out for too long, but I wanted to go. I needed some fresh air. When Dad parked the car, we got out and headed towards the restaurant.

I felt ugly. The steroids caused my weight to increase by more than a hundred pounds and I couldn't handle it. My movement appeared to be precisely calculated and somewhat painful with every step. I noticed the eyes of strangers gazing upon me with fear. I think the n95 blue mask covering my mouth frightened them, as the smallest things have a way of causing anxiety in people. In actuality, *I* was terrified of *them* and the threat of their germs causing my frail system to worsen. Being outside of a sterile environment left me taking a substantial risk in a vastly contaminated world. In a matter of minutes, fear and panic surged into my reality. Quickly suppressing it, I continued on to the restaurant. As Dad and I sat down to enjoy dinner with some of our family I found it difficult to relax. I became more uncomfortable at the thought of the impending threats surrounding me. Absolutely petrified, I got up and left the restaurant at a slow but steady pace once this little boy started belting out a line of heavy coughing. Ironically, the only place I felt completely safe was the hospital.

When I returned home I headed straight for my bedroom, shut the door and curled up in bed. I stared at the walls until I got lost in a pool of desolate thoughts. I was out of time and I felt it. Cancer was erasing me. I never felt I *fit* in this world and if they didn't find a match soon, life was going to confirm what I'd always felt. I said in a low whisper, "*Please, there must be someone out there who can save me.*"

I reached for my headphones, grabbed the remote and turned on the music. Anger and bitterness inhabited my soul while the music quickly infiltrated my mind. I closed my eyes tightly and let it take me. It had become easy for me to think negative thoughts when my life was being eaten away in front of everyone I loved. This time, my music was dark.

In April of 2007, I had complications due to the chemo and needed to remain in the hospital overnight. Later the next afternoon, my oncologist walked into my room with an unusual look of relief washed across her face. As she reviewed my test results she released a slight smile. I didn't know why she was smiling because I wasn't feeling any better. She looked at Mum, Dad, Jen and then me before pleasantly announcing, "We didn't think we'd find a match for you." After a short pause she added, "Instead, we've found *two* perfect matches for your bone marrow transplant. David, you can pick whichever donor you want!"

For a few seconds it appeared as though no one heard what she said. Each of us displayed an awkward silence until her words registered. The prevailing worried expressions from my family cautiously shifted and then the three of them reveled in optimism, at least for my benefit. Utter shock hit me the same way it had everyone else, yet I remained inexpressive and somewhat out of sorts because of the drugs and the fact I'd been emotionally numb for so long. I raised my hand to my mouth and began biting my fingernails. It sounded implausible to hear the doctor explain I had *two* bone marrow matches after all this time and perpetual skepticism.

Everyone waited for my reaction. I wanted to express some sort of excitement except, nothing came out. I didn't know what to say because I'd anticipated death for so long. Having a reaction to something this significant never came under consideration because it wasn't expected. I hadn't given up hope; it was just hard to forget about death because it wouldn't stop pilfering and feasting on pieces of me. Every time I glanced at my reflection I could see death smiling back at me as though it were winning. It was, because I could feel the cancer devouring me. That's what it does.

I had to shove that negativity aside and deal with the facts. After months of waiting to die in what felt like an isolated holding cell, *I had a donor*! Actually, I had two donors and my doctor let me select which one *I* wanted. At the very moment I no longer believed in it, *hope showed up!*

One of the donors had a blood type that was B+. *Be positive* had been my mantra thus far and I liked the way it sounded. I selected the donor based on their blood type. Since being diagnosed with leukemia it remained imperative for me to, *be positive.* Even when I wasn't, I had to force myself to return to a positive state as quickly as possible before more damage ensued.

I hadn't acquired a single bit of information about the donor. Yet, someone in this world actually thought I was worthy of having a second chance at life. They didn't know anything about me other than I was a human being in need of *their* bone marrow and if I didn't get it, *I'd die*. The donor was sympathetic to the fact; he or she had something vital to keep another person alive and was willing to donate it. *The donor wanted me to live.*

A donor has compassion, which extends beyond the boundaries of life and blocks the door to death for those not ready to walk through it. Donors want to help people fighting a disease or illness to stay alive because they have respect for life and feel it is the right thing to do. They are extraordinarily selfless individuals.

I took a deep breath and exhaled slowly while positioning myself in bed. As my lips began to quiver my vision flooded with heavy tears. I couldn't wrap my senses around someone thinking *I* had any kind of value to this world. As the doctor waited for a response, I managed a voiceless affirmation offering an awkward grin and an appreciative short nod of my head. I was humbled. I knew it was essential for me to meet the individual with this kind of generosity towards a stranger. I knew at some point I'd have to look into their eyes and let my heart say, thank you.

Anxious to know the specifics about this person, I began asking questions. The doctor stated their identity and location, as well as mine, would remain confidential until some time had passed and it was mutual we wanted to communicate with one another. She wasn't at liberty to tell me anything further.

The next day, I was released to go home until my bone marrow transplant, scheduled a few weeks later. If successful, it would save my life but the process involved more than the transplant. My body needed to accept it. I didn't move away from being terrified because they told me I had a sixty percent chance of dying. It was hard to get those odds out of my head. I didn't do well on tests and was all too familiar with that percentage along with the grade. It left me with enough room for *hope* but not energy for a celebration, at least not yet.

The doctors weren't optimistic about the bone marrow taking because of my poor health history but it was the only thing left for them to do. This transplant was their last attempt. My oncologist wanted me to understand my reality so she spoke to me from the facts and statistics in my charts, not from what they thought. At this stage, they considered I may have been too far-gone and I felt like it.

Two weeks later I was back in the hospital being prepped for my transplant scheduled the beginning of May 2007. I had an extremely thorough examination. They completed several different tests and scans to check the condition of my liver, heart, lungs and other internal organs. Since beginning treatment, I'd taken so many types of medications they needed to make sure I didn't have any additional damage because of them. If I did, they had to determine the severity. They made certain my organs were healthy enough to withstand the medicines they'd prescribe to help with recovery. The transplant would unquestionably put me at high-risk for infection so I couldn't afford to have underlying issues they weren't aware of.

The day of my bone marrow transplant, my oncologist confidently walked into the crowded hospital room and explained the entire process again. The stem cells were harvested from my healthy donor, which meant I was having an allogeneic transplantation. She said they were going to hang the bag of bone marrow, allowing it to drip into my Hickman line and make it's way into my body like a blood transfusion. The process was going to be slow, however it would be painless. I had to wait for the stem cells to reach my bone marrow and begin producing new blood cells. After that, it would take one hundred days before I'd know if the transplant took. I'd remain in the hospital so they could closely monitor me for any complications, rejection of the bone marrow or side effects during my recovery. Mum, Dad, Jen and a lot of friends and family were anxious for me to get my life back. I could see a glimmer of encouragement returning to my sister's beautiful eyes. I could feel the hope.

My addiction caused me to have a lower threshold for pain so I was given a lot of post transplant pain medications. Fearful of the outcome, I adjusted the pillow, sat back and let my eyes follow the slow drip as it began. I needed to believe. Silently hoping that the bone marrow transplant would take, I begged for every little drop filtering into my body to fill me with life, but no one knew it.

After the transplant, remaining in the hospital was difficult. We were held captive to time and impatiently waited for the results to see if anything would change. My fate wasn't in my hands, but in the bone marrow donated by a stranger with incomparable kindness.

One hundred days later I left the hospital and returned home. The bone marrow transplant had taken! Given the physical destruction cancer rendered to my body, it was a miracle I survived. The gratitude to my family, the team of doctors and my donor couldn't be put into words. I was gifted another chance at life.

The same way summer makes its return to Canada, I relaxed on my sofa and listened to a selection of music beginning with The Traveling Wilbury's, George Harrison and Tom Petty, then I went *above the clouds*. The music unlocked the gate and my memories boldly returned. I tried to recall the moment my life became as black as an abyss and threatened by the invisible mist of death. I should have seen the warning signs because they were there. Regrettably, I dismissed some and minimized others. I thought I had the flu.

Chapter 14

Symptoms

Many seasons passed since our family was whole and I found myself going through the empty motions while uncomfortably settled into my life, relationship and all. It became an enigma as to the reason I remained in Ft. McMurray when I was able to move anywhere, especially knowing how much I loved Manchester. I established a few solid friendships and traveled quite a bit; taking sight of some incredible places. Somehow, I always returned to the only home I knew, which is where Dad lived.

I felt sorry for Dad. He stayed in Ft. McMurray working diligently, executing plans to develop his businesses while looking after Jen and I. Due to his family ties and ongoing success, when I thought of Ft. McMurray, it remained synonymous with Dad. He grew up in Ft. Chipewyan or Ft. Chip as it's known, and maintained strong ties to his origin.

Mum still lived in England and although I didn't think her visits would wane any more than they had, they did. Somehow, I found it convenient to return to my anger after being away from her for several months. Anger and I had become rather acquainted with one another so I used it to protect myself. I missed Mum and expressing it wasn't enough to bring her back so I boxed up my private anguish and tucked it away as neatly as I could. By default, her absence pushed me closer to Dad. I never told him but I was grateful he was there for me.

I slowed down a bit but had too much time on my hands. It wasn't good because I searched for unhealthy ways to suppress my mental anguish and physical pain. My body hurt and I'd become emotionally unstable. I didn't think Dad noticed the changes with me, but he did. He just wasn't sure how to address it. My father worked obsessively and continued to be an incredible provider, but he didn't have time to analyze the reasons I tried to smother my pain. I'm sure he didn't have a notion where it stemmed from either. Mum wasn't around enough to sense the severity, but she absolutely knew something was wrong.

By the spring of 2005, years after high school, my routine hadn't changed all too much. I was bored. Music and partying had become part of my daily routine. I didn't have anything significant to occupy my days, which caused my use of time to become unproductive. Indicative of my emotional state, my mind persistently drifted away with soul-crushing music because its lyrics often described me.

Skeptical it would actually come to fruition, I thought about opening some type of business. I didn't have any purpose or meaning and needed to find a constructive outlet for my creativity. There were days I couldn't manage to pull myself together for anything. I didn't feel well and considered the cause to be my lack of accomplishing anything. I was depressed and needed something to help revitalize me.

Like my father, Canada had taken root a little deeper in me and I considered opening a coffee shop in Westbank, British Columbia near Jen. Dad and I discussed the possibility and he thought it to be a great idea. Sensing I wasn't in a good place, Dad was willing to do anything to help motivate me. Owning a coffee shop wasn't exactly my passion but I settled for it because I thought it would be the closest I'd get to being surrounded by music. Having my own shop would allow me to offer great service, in a comfortable environment, while playing an eclectic selection of soul-stirring music. I wanted to blend all the elements of music I loved most and share them with the clientele. The coffee had to be pretty awesome too. We did the research and Dad started the process.

Late fall presented the blustery imprint of winter being distributed quite generously. I forced myself to get out of bed that day because I needed to run a few errands. From the moment I stepped outside, I wished I hadn't. The frigid temperature slapped me a little harder that morning and then whipped across my feverish body. I finished running around by late afternoon just as darkness cleverly claimed the sky. I desired to be back in the comfort of my bed but since I was in the vicinity of Dad's office I thought I'd stop in to see him. I turned the corner, pulled into Tuccaro Inc.'s lot and parked the car. Before getting out, I tried to catch my breath and gather my composure. I reached into the glove compartment and pulled out a couple of white tissues. Adjusting the mirror on the visor, I dabbed away the stained blood inside the edge of my left nostril from the nosebleed I had twenty-minutes earlier. It was bad. When I dragged myself into Dad's office, he took a really hard look at me. He wouldn't take his eyes off of me and his facial expression displayed an unembellished look of concern. He studied me for a few minutes before communicating how awful I looked. What he didn't know was that I'd been feeling run down and unusually sick for several weeks. I positioned myself in the chair in front of his desk and explained why I looked so poorly. I felt like I was fighting a really bad flu but couldn't manage to shake it off.

    My body ached right down to my bones. Only a few weeks prior I started having little black and white floaters in my vision that were quite distracting. I struggled to describe them to Dad and had previously explained it to Jen, but like my sister, he didn't seem to understand. I tried to convey how the floaters appeared indiscriminately, completely clouding my vision at times. The strangest thing about my body happened to be a constant vibration radiating throughout, coupled with a sharp, stabbing pain on my left side, which frequently became crippling. I'd lie down and curl up into a tight fetal position wading in insufferable agony waiting for it to dissipate. It usually took hours before subsiding. It became impossible to sleep at night because of the constant aching and heavy night sweats. Overloaded with fatigue, I didn't have the energy to do anything except lie around and listen to music. There were times I could barely stand up because a languid feeling swooned comfortably inside of my sick body making me weak. Without warning, I ran high fevers that were random but consistent in their return. If I so much as bumped any part of my limbs on anything it caused bleeding under my skin and eventually left unsightly bruising like I'd been in a fight. I tried to tell Dad about everything that had been going on and nearly forgot my recurring nosebleeds. The long-winded narration resulted in the ragged compilation sitting in front of Dad.

Dad carefully studied my frail face again as an even graver look of concern descended to the surface of his and rested in his serious eyes. He clasped his hands together and authoritatively instructed me to make an immediate appointment to be seen by the doctor. Dad wasn't asking me to go, he told me to. His concern worried me, so without protest I went.

After a brief exchange of words with my doctor, nothing other than a prescription for Pantoloc came of it because I told him it may have been an ulcer. He conceded without taking any blood work or running tests. I went about my usual routine taking the ulcer medication until a week later when things progressively grew worse. The nosebleeds became more persistent and I couldn't manage to keep anything down. I believed this to be the worst form of the flu anyone could possibly have. Without further consideration to my many symptoms, neglectfully I dismissed all of them.

My vinyl record collection represented an impressive résumé of music history. It was a phenomenal anthology and I didn't like being too far away from it unless absolutely necessary. I had the best compilation of classic rock, metal, hip-hop and techno, in addition to, a repertoire of other great music in between.

Since I was preparing to relocate near Jen in Westbank, due to my extreme love of music, I had about six hundred vinyl records to move. Although the boxes were ridiculously heavy, I was used to lugging them around. Oddly, that time, I could barely lift them. I had no other alternative than to bend over and push them along the snow-covered path until I reached the truck. Each time I lifted a box it felt like it was jam-packed with kryptonite, which quickly depleted my energy. The temperature was so cold that it wasn't logical for me to be soaked in sweat and burning up. I felt like I was on fire. I fell back onto a high bank of snow, allowing my body to slowly sink in a couple inches so I'd cool off. I packed a huge chunk of powder in my hand and then rubbed it all over my face and neck. I put my hand over my brow as if saluting the sun to block the glare. I stared at the vibrant blue sky residing above me and silently acknowledged that I was scared.

December 20, 2006 brought the usual anticipated thrashing of intense cold into Ft. McMurray. Unfortunately, where I was headed wouldn't be any better. I had already postponed two flights earlier that morning. I couldn't make it to the airport because I didn't feel well so I rescheduled. Several hours later, I made another attempt and caught a couple flights to Westbank. I wanted to spend the holiday with my sister.

When I got off the plane in Calgary, I struggled to walk through the airport corridor. I had an indescribable discomfort that resonated in my bones. Tiny white dots and black floaters clouded my vision again. Staggering as though intoxicated, I made my way over to a seat along a wall. Completely depleted, I plopped down and rested until I gained enough energy to grab something to eat. I suspected my severe anemia dragged me to that exhaustive state. I managed to get lunch, but as soon as I took the first bite I was forced to turn my head away from the food to avoid the smell, which made me ill. I left the rest of my meal on the table and struggled to get up. It was an unbelievable feat just to make it to the gate because I had physically deteriorated beyond my control. Perspiration covered my face and dripped down my body underneath my clothing. When the final announcement for the flight to Kelowna was given, I boarded the plane with serious reservations about going.

I knew the Pantoloc wasn't working and I thought the problem with my exhaustion might have been a result of the excessive bleeding when I went to the bathroom. I remained persistent in assuming it was an ulcer bleeding out. I thought it only made sense that the loss of blood caused my anemia to worsen. I didn't have time to worry about it being anything else so I kept dismissing it. I considered myself too young for it to be anything significant.

When my sister picked me up from the airport I asked her to stop at a store. I wanted to buy some iron tablets, hoping they would correct my energy deficiency. When I returned to the car, I took three or four of the tablets thinking they would help. As soon as Jen pulled into her driveway, I flung open the door, stepped out the car and hurled all over her driveway. Jen was visibly upset about the mess. Feeling like death was tugging at me, I went inside and rested on the sofa. This wasn't a good way to start what was meant to be an enjoyable holiday visit.

Mum was already at Jen's because we decided to spend Christmas together. A slight tension filtered between us but I was happy to see Mum. I looked forward to enjoying a few of her delicious meals while catching up on some much needed rest. The timing seemed perfect.

The heavy snow painted the remarkable scenery outdoors but I could barely stand up straight to enjoy the view. Something wasn't right. Everything about me was changing and I didn't like the transformation. I had the constant infliction of agony, but no one seemed to notice. I rested my two hundred and eighty-five pound frame on the sofa attempting to wait out the pain on my left side. It felt like I was being stabbed with a searing hot, steel hunter's knife. I let out several unnoticed agonizing grunts and uncontrolled grimaces to keep from outright screaming but no one responded. Nothing I did helped, so I curled myself into a tight fetal position and sheathed my abdomen with my arms to restrict the pain from spreading. My eyes were tightly closed as I struggled to fight through it. It seemed as though Mum and Jen considered my illness undoubtedly a side effect of my recreational reveling in drugs. I owned their assessment because I wasn't entirely sure it didn't have something to do with what I was dealing with.

I had no idea what was happening to me. The severity of my symptoms let me know it wasn't the flu because they persisted for over six weeks. My body became exhausted and I desperately needed sleep. Without saying much else, I gradually climbed the stairs and went to bed.

From the time I opened my weary eyes the next morning, I knew it was going to be another rough one. Christmas was only two days away and I felt like death. I didn't attempt to get out of bed until ten-thirty because my body wouldn't allow it. When I gathered the strength to take a shower, it took a long time to make my way into the bathroom only a few yards away. The feeling of walking the length of a football field, from one goal post to the other, is what I experienced. With sluggish movements and aching joints, I stepped into the shower. I carefully bent down to pick up the shampoo and when I stood up, the curtain dropped and everything went black.

When I came to, I found myself lying in a stream of bright red blood. The cold water flowed over my body washing the blood from my nose. I had a sizable lump, which indicated that I hit my head. As I lifted it, more blood flushed from beneath. I got out of the shower and tried to stop my nose from bleeding. For some reason, it took nearly thirty minutes. I took this as a warning.

I was so exhausted it took me over an hour before I got dressed. My energy rapidly decreased like a battery that hadn't been charged long enough. I'd lie across the bed and attempt to reenergize but the process was slow. As soon as I thought I mustered enough energy, I'd struggle to put on an article of clothing before lying down to collect a little more strength. I repeated the cycle until I was finally dressed.

I never considered walking down a flight of stairs could turn into such a massive journey. Gripping the rail, I struggled down the first two steps before having to sit down and rest. I'd slowly manage another step and then find myself unable to continue without a break. By the time I reached the bottom of the stairs I found Mum and Jen doing all of the preparations for Christmas and they were noticeably upset with me because I hadn't helped. Jen looked at my intentionally slow and lethargic movements like I was being weird. I didn't say anything because I didn't want to argue. I needed to rest.

I could tell Mum's eyes were keenly observing me. With certainty, she suspected something was wrong. Nonetheless, she didn't respond. Instead, she acted as if this type of behavior was typical. She made her way into the kitchen and finished prepping for dinner. I wanted to do something to help out, but didn't have the physical capability to sustain moving around for too long. I staggered over to the sofa to lie down hoping I'd feel better and closed my eyes. Shortly after, Jen began complaining that I wasn't doing anything to help and insisted I make myself useful. She didn't understand the severity of my illness and I couldn't make her, so after some coaxing from Jen, we went to the local store to pick up a few groceries.

Once we made it inside the store, I felt like someone flipped a switch and I turned off. I could hardly stand. Rather upset, Jen proceeded with the shopping as I rested on a bench, waiting for her. When she finished checking out, I told her I didn't feel well. She loaded the groceries into the jeep, and ignoring my protest, proceeded to the Real Canadian Superstore. I struggled to trail behind her, sluggishly dragging myself up and down the isles. My vision became clouded with white dots and black floaters. The floaters randomly came into view and flashed away without warning. Overcome with confusion and fear I tried to stand still and pull myself together. I'd become so discombobulated it didn't rectify the problem. Without warning, a scathing pain slowly crawled up my spine causing a nearly immobilizing sensation of agony. I wanted to scream. Barely able to walk, I stumbled as though I was completely inebriated. My eyesight failed and I could scarcely see anything. It took nearly an hour before we left the store due to my inability to move normally in addition to the rising motion of nausea threatening me.

By the time we loaded the groceries into the jeep and returned home, it was shortly after five-thirty that evening. Mum helped Jen unpack the groceries while I dropped back down on the sofa in an uncontrolled plunge and gazed lifelessly at the television.

Minutes later, Mum and Jen were sitting at the table. They wanted to play a board game and Jen insisted I play a round or two. When I stood up, I couldn't walk without holding onto the furniture, trying to make my way over to the table. I didn't want to participate because I was sick and aggravated that they didn't believe me. I sat down to play, but intentionally lost so I could end the game and lie back down. Mum's facial expressions couldn't hide her irritation. She was still fighting not to say anything. It was obvious they thought I didn't want to be bothered because I was stoned out of my mind.

At that point, the only sympathy I received came from the two English pitbull's Otis and Paris. They came over to me and rather compassionately, licked my face. Otis climbed on the sofa and rested his head on my shoulder while Paris sat right next to me. They knew something was wrong.

Ultimately, Jen couldn't take anymore of my odd behavior and snapped at me pretty bad. Afterwards, she and Mum got up from the table and went into the kitchen to secretly converse. When they returned to the living room, they insisted on taking me to the hospital or said they'd call an ambulance. The pain was intolerable and I needed help because I wasn't in any position to object. After putting on my coat and boots, I took slow careful movements to the jeep and climbed inside as if one slight bump or fall would break me. My mind drifted deep into thought while I cast an unresponsive stare out the window while tapping nervously on my leg.

Mum walked over to the registration desk and checked me in. Using my sister and the chairs for stability to walk, I found a place to rest my body while preparing for a lengthy wait. The nurse came over and took my temperature rather expeditiously. Upon discovering my dangerously high fever they took me in the back without delay and commenced checking the rest of my vitals. The phlebotomist came in to draw blood on three separate occasions and sent it to the lab. After the first two draws, I was told my white blood cell count was climbing. As soon as it came back a third time the doctor entered the room and said I had the second highest white blood cell elevation in the providence of British Columbia. The doctor wouldn't communicate anything further until the rest of my testing was completed. I didn't know what a high white blood cell count was indicative of, but I determined it couldn't have been favorable.

There was a guy in the bed next to me. I don't know why he was there but the loud piercing cries coming from behind the curtain were awful. I felt bad for him. I knew I was sick yet; I couldn't help to think, that guy had it worse.

I was hoping the doctors would do whatever they deemed necessary so I could get better and return to Jen's. Mum and my sister appeared to be in agreement. Christmas was on its way and I didn't want to disrupt everyone's holiday. None of us wanted to be there. Regrettably, I was cognizant the hospital was the only place I belonged.

I lifted my right hand to my mouth and began biting my fingernails. I needed to ease the heavy apprehension steadily emerging. I closed my eyes and sang to myself, *I don't see nothing new but I feel a lot of change.* I had no idea how much my life was about to change.

Chapter 15

The Gift

I stepped onto the patio inhaling a liberal breath of fresh air as the summer breeze gently swept past me. I glanced around and took in all of the magnificence surrounding me. I beat it! I'd been gifted a second chance at life and it humbled me.

I wasn't without numerous regrets because I didn't make complete use of the gift the first time around. Now, I had another opportunity to make it right. Countless people will continue to lose their battle until a cure is found or generous donors like mine, offer their gift of life. Deliberating over the widespread devastation cancer brings caused a stream of tears to fall down my cheeks.

I didn't pick this fight with cancer. I tried my best to stay out of everyone's path but this disease bullied me right up to the gripping conclusion. In some respects, it's still taunting me, but I won't give in.

I thought I'd get my life back after the first one hundred days of having the transplant, but that wasn't the case. I had to move forward, living one day at a time, as an addict. I made the choice to use drugs the year prior to my diagnosis to dull some of my emotional and then physical pain. After the diagnosis of leukemia, relying on pain medication for years became another destructive part of my life that seemed unavoidable. Being cognizant I could die at any moment caused me not to give credence to what the drugs were doing to me. I developed a serious dependency with the prescription pain medications and dilaudid, in particular. Quite honestly, my body needed them and I wasn't willing to stop. At one point during my treatment, I was taking over fifty pills per day aware of the detrimental side effects.

The drugs and treatments for leukemia were one thing but everything else was given to counter the side effects and damage being done by the others.

My treatment consisted of six rounds of radiation and two rounds of intense chemo. While my bone marrow transplant was a huge success for the simple fact that I'm alive, leukemia made sure it left its detectable marks all over my body and invaded my future. I was ridden with several debilitating repercussions, which caused a considerable change in the quality of my life. My oncologist was amazing but she remained a realist based on the evidence in front of her. She didn't show a great deal of sympathy but her passion for her work saved my life. It was her unremitting regimen and advice that I followed.

A year after the surgery I'd lost forty pounds by eating healthy and regaining mobility. But over time, I couldn't handle the pain from walking and often used a wheelchair when I went out. It didn't take long before the damage from the treatments and medications caused my hips to practically crumble like chalk. In January 2008, I had my right hip replaced and by October the same year, I had the left done. Both hips are made of porcelain.

The damage didn't stop there. By 2009, I think Mum, Dad and Jen realized I was an addict. Dad spent enough time with me to discern the significant changes and depressive modes along with the highs and lows. He said I was completely hollow inside and when he looked at me there was nothing there. It ripped Dad apart to watch me destroy myself. I'm not sure if he understood why, but it didn't seem to matter. It was unthinkable to allow this destruction to occur after such a grueling life-threatening fight.

I took pills every chance I could because I was dependent upon the drugs initially dumped into my system to help with pain management. Since being diagnosed with leukemia, I'd taken dilaudid for practically three and a half years with a prescription so it was nearly impossible to avoid an addiction. I was given a free pass to take whatever I wanted because I was dying so pain medications were easily attainable. The thought of, *what if David survives* never really occurred. When they sent me home post-transplant, the reason was so I would die comfortably.

I'd beaten leukemia, but needed to acknowledge I was in remission. Remission meant I beat it *for now* and the possibility of its return was lurking about. Other serious health conditions plagued me and required ongoing medical treatment. It didn't make sense to survive a formidable battle; yet, become unable to beat an addiction. I was alive but once again, barely existing. I didn't like it although I loved the drugs and I didn't possess the fortitude to fight.

Cancer savagely stripped me of everything and contemptuously contributed to my addiction.

Eventually, Dad refused to ignore my problem any longer. I was withdrawn, irritable, depressed and craved drugs even when I didn't want them. He didn't know what to do but it was killing him to see me afflicted with an addiction and I'm positive it did the same to Mum. Dad asked Jen to help him find a rehab because he didn't want me to die, let alone, this way.

There came a point I decided I wanted to live in California. After years of enduring piercing cold temperatures, the weather alone was reason enough. I wanted to enjoy the sun for more than a few hours each day and break away from the expected darkness in which I found an unhealthy solitude. The constant absence of light continuously fed me depressive thoughts. I wanted to hear the rhythmic pounding of the waves crashing against the shore and walk on sand instead of snow. I didn't feel alive and that was my way of searching for life.

In my sober moments I'd often express how I felt about living in California to Jen. For some reason, it stayed with her. In an effort to encourage me to get help, she found a rehab in Laguna Beach, California. Naturally, I was apprehensive about going to rehab because I'd watched quite a few television shows that executed some serious interventions. I didn't desire to take any part in that. After what I crammed into my body, getting it out was going to be painstaking.

The conversation between my sister and I in regards to rehab turned out to be fairly intense. Just talking about it became agitating to me. I didn't want to be an addict. I didn't try to hurt my family either. I just couldn't stop but I needed to try.

I had a few fleeting thoughts about going to rehab but I wasn't sure how I'd manage my pain if I did. The recovery aspect would be both painful and difficult, which were two things I was familiar with so I kept putting it off. One night Jen and I were out on her balcony discussing whether or not I'd actually go. When I told her, I didn't want to be another rehab statistic, in the most innocent tone she said, "David, it's not rehab. It's a place to rehabilitate yourself." Totally amused by Jen's passionate statement, I burst out laughing. It wasn't an easy thing to do but I accepted the personal challenge and went.

Whenever you're making an investment to destroy yourself, trying to repair the damage is going to take even more work. Regardless of how many times I failed, I believed putting forth the effort until it worked was better than never trying at all. I made the move to California in 2009 and a substantial part of my healing began.

I attempted rehab but it was more like a celebrity playhouse. The bottom-line was it didn't work because I wasn't committed. You have to be present to make changes or improvements in your life and I hadn't shown up.

I took advantage of being in California and relocated to Orange County where I met a doctor with an interesting approach to medicine. After an extensive conversation with him, I believed he could actually help me, *if* I let him. His innovative holistic approach to health care was what I needed. I was tired of everything going into my body and then having to deal with the ugly side effects and toxins killing me.

After meeting with my father, Dr. Gary Ruelas took me on as a patient. The doctors in Canada continued monitoring my health, since I was in remission. I needed something to work because I was completely dismantled emotionally and had trouble getting around due to physical limitations. Lonely and lacking self-confidence, I didn't know how to take control of my life.

No one understood what cancer ripped from me and it seemed as though I had everything back, but I didn't. I felt less than what I did before, which wasn't much. My kidneys were failing and heading straight towards dialysis. I didn't want to continue living out the *Never-ending David Tuccaro Story*. It would have been arduous for anyone to handle another battle with me because the first one was enough. They had their own lives and were forced into mine for far too long. They needed to resume living instead of dying with me.

I convinced myself I couldn't handle anything else so I jumped out of reality, dove into my music and emotionally checked out. Inside of music was where I spent most of my time since there wasn't much I could do elsewhere. I was alive in there but emotionally dead outside. I desperately needed help for what seemed like an *untreatable disease.*

Thankfully my health care shifted over to more of a holistic approach that helped me transition to where I am now. I was twenty-eight years old when I met Dr. Ruelas in the beginning of August 2009. My therapy with him began the following month. When he first met me, I was overweight and in a wheelchair. Debilitated and weak, I needed assistance walking. My mental state was quite depressed and I was still taking several medications;

I wasn't cognizant of much nor did I feel anything. I lived in a constant state of nothingness that I needed to climb out of.

Dr. Ruelas started by working his way through the ugly details of my life. Sometimes I'd talk with him and others, I'd scarcely utter a few sentences. I was cautiously trying to figure him out and ascertained he was doing the same with me. He quickly determined exactly what I needed; however, I wasn't easy to help because I didn't want it. My family wanted me to get better. Whether or not they realized it; I loved them enough to try.

Dr. Ruelas showed genuine concern for my emotional state instead of just the biological part. He knew if he didn't help me get out of this dire emotional state, he wouldn't be able to help me. His first initiative was to begin with therapy and so the connection began. He worked with my oncologist in Canada, analyzing the medications I was taking to help strategically decrease them. He focused on my solid history of depression taking note of the steady decline. I appreciated that his approach included making conscious efforts to be in contact with my family. It was as if he needed to understand them to better understand and help me. *He was right.* After spending additional time with my family Dr. Ruelas knew they had a deep sense of helplessness and frustration with themselves. They desperately wanted to save me, however, they weren't equipped to handle a problem as substantial as I'd become. Dr. Ruelas understood that Mum, Dad and Jen wanted me to get better so they could all get better too. He taught me to understand, healing was critical to making me whole. I had to be willing to heal.

Dr. Ruelas removed all of the labels I'd been given by doctors and threw them away. He became a catalyst for me to fight through this battle but I had to put in the work. The process took time because it was essential to build trust, and we did. Afterwards, he began removing several layers of pain that weighed heavily on me for what seemed like the majority of my lifetime. His therapy was a different type of medicine that nurtured my soul and prepared me to feel whole. He invested time in knowing me instead of my disease and was able to uncouple what my tumultuous journey had encumbered me with. Then, he explained that I was more than my journey. Those were places I've visited and stories of my past but they are not who I am. I was not meant to stay that way, in those places or live in the misery it brought. He worked diligently to empower and rejuvenate my cells, restore my kidney function and help me systematically, do better and better with continued treatment.

Dr. Ruelas took a different approach to his method of treatment, which was through integrative medicine. The areas of his medical expertise are preventive, nutritional, addiction and mental health treatment. His perspective of how he views his patients is unique and somewhat innovative. Dr. Ruelas doesn't see me purely through the lens of a dysfunctional organ system, as a disease, or a syndrome. By evaluating a matrix of root causes in the diagnostic and therapeutic process, he opened my eyes to different ways of thinking about complex and chronic states of stress so he could restore my optimal physical and mental health. Dr. Ruelas pulled my family together and made them aware of what he felt I needed so my treatment would be most effective. It was refreshing to have someone that not only understood me but also advocated for me.

Before Dr. Ruelas could commence with his method of treatment, he had to build me back up, which was going to take a lot of work. He knew how broken I was. I continued meeting him for therapy, pain medication and management a couple times a week. It didn't take long before he became aware I had a number of factors working against me and that I wasn't a typical case. Upon analyzing my records, he noticed my already extensive medication list was continuing to expand in my doctor's efforts to stabilize me. Nevertheless, it wouldn't do me any good if my white blood cells and platelets count was okay, and the leukemia stable, but I was falling apart. My issues with pain were affecting my platelet count and Dr. Ruelas was able to discern my problem was an addiction issue. I was one of his most challenging patients and the fact that I'm alive is a miracle in itself.

In the interim, my family wouldn't give up even if I had. They knew they could lose me and refused to stand by and let it happen. I had a major intervention causing me to make the decision to attend Betty Ford. I didn't want to go but my life depended upon it and the treatment with Dr. Ruelas encompassed treating the addiction. It took a serious commitment and substantial effort on my part to make it work. Betty Ford's structured program offered precisely what an addict needs, *reality*.

Dr. Ruelas analyzed all of my records and detected the substantial increase in my weight. Through testing, he found me to be considerably toxic and with numerous issues he needed to resolve. He took time to go inside of me and realize the root of my problems and found I was afraid of my own power. The thing no one seemed to fully understand except Dr. Ruelas was that I carried the burden of several people and I had done so for a very long time. They weren't the blame for my addiction but contributed to my pain. He wanted me to get better, not only for the leukemia to move past remission but also for me to become whole again.

Dr. Ruelas started giving me the right nutrients to rebuild my brain cells. He believed, unless we were able to get my mind right with the medicine, the medicine wouldn't work. There had to be connections with the mind and the body, but at that time, I didn't have one to either. He had a task on hand and for years Dr. Ruelas worked diligently to connect the mind and body. That process had to come into balance and is where my healing began to truly take place. He works with me in a holistic approach on a regular basis and I'm much healthier because of it. He was able to circumvent my need for dialysis through his method of treatment. He carefully directed my path so I'd avoid additional problems.

Listening and then understanding someone alone can make the difference in helping them. If you don't know an individuals motivation for their decisions, then I don't believe you can help them. Dr. Ruelas took the time to understand why I was self-destructive so he could help me.

My degenerative bones continued to affect my body and by February 2010 I had my left shoulder replaced. Although I beat cancer, it was still beating the hell out of me but I decided *any day above ground was a good one*. I continue to see Dr. Ruelas and sought treatment for my addiction at Betty Ford. I wanted my life back and not just part of it, all of it! I knew it was going take my participation so I joined the fight. I didn't need my life to be pieced back together; I needed to create a healthier lifestyle and environment then live in that one.

Chapter 16

The Miracle

After my transplant, I attempted to obtain my donor's information hoping he or she would want to meet me, but to no avail. I submitted a letter with my contact information so if the donor was ever interested in knowing who I was they could reach me. Unfortunately, when I moved to California a few years later that made it more challenging to be found. Over four years had gone by and the compassion my donor displayed never left me; it's in my blood.

In 2011, I was casually reading through my messages on Facebook and received one from a man named, Christian Holtmann. As soon as I began reading the first few words, my eyes widened and my heart began racing. I couldn't believe it. Christian was my bone marrow donor!

Overwhelmed with excitement I sent Christian an immediate response. I'd waited years just to express my infinite gratitude and until now, lost hope it would happen. As I sat at my computer, nervously tapping my fingers to the music playing in my head, I waited for a response. When it arrived, I learned that Christian's bone marrow came all the way from Bünde, Germany. There was so much I wanted to know about him that my fingers couldn't type fast enough to keep up with the questions emerging in my head. Using an online translator, we began communicating very well and he freely allowed me to ask him anything. The first thing I wanted to know was how he became my donor. Christian revealed his incredible account from the very beginning.

In December of 2006, Christian Holtmann received a letter from Delete Blood Cancer DKMS. When he opened the letter it stated, it had been determined he was a match for a patient needing a stem cell donor. In complete disbelief, Christian explained his response was, "The DKMS and their foreign counterparts have several million pieces of information with data containing blood tests in their database, and they've calculated that *my* blood is a match for someone, somewhere in this world!"

Nearly three and a half years prior, a suitable bone marrow donor was being sought for Christian's wife's four-year-old cousin. It wasn't until that particular incident he'd ever known exactly what leukemia was, but it didn't matter. Christian believed when something in the family happens, albeit by marriage, you're supposed to pull together and do something about it. Without hesitation, he registered to become a donor.

Unfortunately, Christian's blood wasn't a match. However, due to the generosity and compassion of another bone marrow donor his cousin had a successful transplant.

Too often, we don't realize the powerful gifts we possess. We're not aware that something like the soft spongy tissue inside of our bones has the ability to save someone's life. Being a donor may not be significant to you but it's a matter of life and death to the person in need, as I was and Christian's little cousin. To have it gifted to us is invaluable.

Christian couldn't believe he was standing there holding a letter stating his tissue was a *fit* for another human being and it was possible he could save their life. He was overwhelmed by an incredible but strange feeling of joy. He didn't know what to expect and had several questions he was eager to ask. Of course, the first thing he wanted to know was, "Who is the patient?"

He called the DKMS to find out what the next steps were. They told him, before any information about the recipient could be provided, several things needed to occur. They wanted him to provide them with a written confirmation stating he agreed to be the donor, which would then begin the process. He was aware time was of the essence and expeditiously began doing everything requested of him.

It had been a few years since Christian became a donor so they needed to make sure he was still a viable candidate. Christian met with his family doctor so they could analyze his blood again. His bloodwork came back showing that according to a majority of votes, he still matched. He was then required to complete a health questionnaire asking typical questions such as height, weight, diseases that either he or immediate relatives, such as his parents, were diagnosed with. Of course, they wanted to know if anyone had cancer. The questions were very thorough and he had to be extremely accurate and completely truthful about every single response as my life depended upon it.

When the questionnaire was completed and approved they allowed him to have a consultation with an expert. Christian was able to ask any questions he had, but he said it didn't matter because he was going to donate regardless. However, at this point, he was able to find out more about the process and how the donation worked. Although he wasn't worried, he inquired about whether or not he would have side effects and then found out what they were. Christian finished his consultation and was ready to save my life. Eager to help me, he asked, "Where do I need to go, to donate?"

They sent him detailed information about the removal clinic in Hameln. He needed to have an ECG, ultrasound, understand critical information about blood loss, and review a lot of information on the preparation for the procedure and the process of the withdrawal.

Christian was ready to make a difference in the life of a complete stranger and excited about moving forward when he received a call from a doctor who asked, "Do you really want to do this?" This was the final moment of his decision. He couldn't understand the question because he knew the person in need of the bone marrow was prepared for the donation and their life depended upon it.

To Christian, the possibility of withdrawing his original decision was not an option and never crossed his mind. With certainty, he wanted to save a life. If Christian said, "Yes," and then changed his decision, he was told, "The patient will not survive." Christian valued my life as much as his own and without vacillation replied, "Yes."

Upon Christian's final decision, my doctors prepared my body for the transplant. My immune system was completely destroyed and I was supposed to get his cells, which were only accepted by my body's defense when the system was suspended. Once this process is done, they warned Christian it cannot be undone easily.

There were two methods of extracting Christian's bone marrow and the final decision rested with him. The procedure Christian chose, gave me the best possible chance at the bone marrow taking. It was like having dialysis. But in order to have the bone marrow in sufficient form in the blood, he had to give himself three injections a day for five consecutive days prior to his donation. He was injecting himself with a protein similar to a hormone naturally produced in the body called, filgrastim. It moves the blood-forming cells out of the marrow and into the bloodstream so there were enough blood-forming cells for the transplant. It stimulated the bone marrow formation from the fourth day prior to the removal. Christian's side effects began on the first day causing symptoms, which mimicked the development of a cold. By the fifth day he had what appeared to be a very bad flu. The night before, the donation, he didn't sleep well. It wasn't because he was afraid; he was excited about having the procedure. Christian, was looking forward to saving my life.

The DKMS put him up in a hotel and the following morning, Christian went to the hospital in Hameln, Germany to provide the donation of his bone marrow. They gave him a simple blood test and then after the results, he was connected to the dialysis machine. Blood was taken from his right arm and passed through a tube system in a machine which Christian said, "His blood was being washed."

Nearly five hours later everything was done. The bag with the bone marrow cells was full and the flu-like side effects were completely gone. During the afternoon, Christian was told the recovered amount of bone marrow was sufficient for the receiver, so he didn't need to go through the process again the next morning. The donation was made and Christian left, not knowing anything about me, my sex, race, religion or anything else. He simply wanted me to live.

A few days later, Christian found out his stem cells were flown to Canada, where a twenty-five-year-old male was waiting for that plastic bag to save his life. No one really hears about the donor or what they unselfishly go through as the end result for the patient seems to be the focus. By all accounts, Christian never took that under consideration. He was concerned with nothing more than saving someone's life.

Both of us knew we needed to wait at least two years before either of us had the option to know anything about the other. I was happy when Christian explained the DKMS called and let him know I was doing okay. That was all they were able to communicate but it was better than nothing. He had no idea I would never receive his contact information nor would he receive mine as it was lost in translation for more than four silent years. I explained to Christian that I believed the donor wanted to stay anonymous.

Christian, remained hopeful throughout the years and continued checking for a letter from the DKMS. On August 17th, 2011 it actually arrived.

Christian said, when the letter came in the mail, "The feeling was indescribable." The letter revealed the information I orginally provided, giving him a place to begin. By that time, I had moved to California a couple years prior. It didn't matter because just as Christian was determined to save my life, he was going to find me.

One of the most significant aspects of this is that Christian didn't speak English and I didn't speak German. Through the power of social media, and online translator options, the language barrier didn't stop him. His passionate search began. After finding my father first, it led him to me, his blood brother. We were destined to meet.

Our conversation was effervescent. He expressed his joy and gratitude to be given the opportunity to help another human being and I was grateful it was me. Everything about our communciation was natural. There was a great deal both of us wanted to know about the other and it seemed the best way to do it would be in person.

My birthday was only a couple weeks away and hoping it was possible, I invited Christian to join my family and I in Las Vegas because the way I saw it, he was family. From the moment I was told I had a donor, I was compelled to express my *undying* appreciation to the person compassionate enough to save my life. I wanted to look into their eyes and thank them with every bit of gratitude inside of me! When Christian agreed to come, I was humbled.

Christian traveled from Germany to Los Angeles and when he got off the plane, Mum, my friend Joseph and fiancee' Cynthia were all waiting with me to greet him. Our excitement was hardly containable. We were standing there holding two big signs written in German, combined with just a little English so he wouldn't have any problems finding us although, I'm not easy to miss. As soon as Christian came through customs I ran over to my genetic twin, grabbed him and thanked him from the best part of my soul. I couldn't express any other emotions because they were simply between brothers.

Christian was about five-foot-ten, had blonde hair, grayish-green eyes and no visible tattoo's. His spirit felt pure and his heart was simply unbelievable. Our language barrier couldn't stop our story from happening and our future bond from lasting. This was our destiny. Christian saved my life and I have tremendous appreciation for him.

I was told it would take a miracle to save my life, and it was standing right in front of me.

Christian Holtmann and his family.

Me and Christian Holtmann,
my bone marrow donor, Summer 2013

Chapter 17

I Am

In August of 2013 I had my entire right knee replaced while the left one remains imminent. I'll have more challenges but I'll work to find ways to handle them. I won't always fit into someone else's world but through building my self-confidence I'm learning to be comfortable in mine. While my battle with leukemia took a lot out of me, in a strange way, like music, it gave me something precious; another way to view and appreciate life.

While it's possible to choose parts of our journey, others will remain unknown and so will life's challenges until they are upon us. I've found Dr. Ruelas is teaching me to prepare for the journey ahead instead of reacting to it. This is a priceless lesson that many of us need to learn.

We are not supposed to let go of the very things that define us and give in to the negative temptations life offers because they will only work to destroy us, if we allow it.

My life has changed and the pain I continue to endure has become a constant part of my life. I am learning to manage it with the proper help from Dr. Ruelas by understanding the ramifications that medications have on the human body. While one is meant to help, another may be given to counter the affects and so on, at times filling our body with toxins that may contribute to our demise emotionally, mentally or physically. Knowledge is power so take time to understand things and the relationships they have, more closely. It can make you aware of the consequences before you are unexpectedly hit with them.

What I've come to realize is that *I am* a miracle. I was given a chance to live, against tremendous odds. I am not supposed to waste the gift of life by destroying it with self-pity, victimizing myself or through fear. I am meant to fight because *I do fit* in this world. Another human being gave up their bone marrow so I could live, proving that my life *does* have value.

Sometimes the journey gets hard and can be long, but looking back, I was never alone thanks to the love of my Mum, Dad, Jen, family, friends, doctors, nurses, and everyone else that fought for me, when I wasn't able to fight for myself.

Leukemia didn't define or destroy me although it is definitely, *Bad to the Bone!*

Become a bone marrow donor today! Give the gift of life as someone's life depends on it.

Afterword

Lieber David!

Es ist noch nicht lange her, dass wir nichts übereinander wussten. Wir waren Fremde, bis uns das Schicksal zusammenbrachte. Es waren ungewisse Zeiten in denen wir an den anderen gedacht haben, aber keine Chance hatten, die Situation zu ändern.

Sehr gerne erinnere ich mich daher an unser erstes Treffen am Flughafen Los Angeles und an die selbstgemalten Schilder, die Du, Cynthia, Joseph und natürlich Deine Mutter Jackie, zu meiner Begrüßung gehalten habt. Dann das Treffen mit Deiner ganzen Familie und die großartige Geburtstagsfeier, bei der es uns an nichts gemangelt hat! Das war eine unbeschreiblich tolle Erfahrung. Ich danke Euch allen dafür!

Es erfüllt mich mit Stolz, einen genetischen Zwilling und Bruder wie Dich zu haben. Ich bewundere die Kraft, mit der Du den Kampf gegen den Blutkrebs kämpfst. Du zeigst anderen Menschen, dass es sich lohnt, für das Leben zu kämpfen.

Unsere gemeinsamen Treffen haben auch mein Leben und die Sicht auf die Dinge, die wirklich wichtig sind, verändert. Ich danke Dir und allen Personen, die uns diese Möglichkeit gegeben haben.

Lieber Bruder, ich freue mich auf die zukünftigen Treffen und die gemeinsamen Zeiten mit Dir und Deiner Familie.

        Christian

Dad, I remember the Pemberton Music Festival. Thanks for always being there when I didn't think you were.

Mum, I never wanted to let go of you because when I didn't have you, my strength and joy disappeared. I was afraid of my own power so I relied on yours.

Jen, the look in your eyes when you talked to me about rehabilitation let me know how much you truly love me. Thank you.

I love you all!

Marala Scott is the Award-winning Author of In Our House: Perception vs. Reality and Surrounded by Inspiration. She is a Motivational Speaker, Ghostwriter and Oprah Winfrey's Ambassador of Hope.

For more information about Marala Scott, please visit: www.maralascott.com

www.ingramcontent.com/pod-product-compliance
Lightning Source LLC
Chambersburg PA
CBHW032123090426
42743CB00007B/435